WILLIAM MALTESE'S WINE TASTER'S DIARY

Spokane and Pullman, Washington

Borgo Press Books by William Maltese:

THE TRAVELING GOURMAND SERIES:

Back of the Boat Gourmet Cooking: Afloat—Pool-Side—Backyard (with Bonnie Clark) (#2)
The Gluten-Free Way: My Way (with Adrienne Z. Milligan) (#1)
William Maltese's Wine Taster's Diary: Spokane and Pullman, Washington (#3)

WILLIAM MALTESE'S WINE TASTER'S DIARY

SPOKANE AND PULLMAN, WASHINGTON

The Traveling Gourmand, Book Three

by

WILLIAM MALTESE

THE BORGO PRESS

An Imprint of Wildside Press LLC

MMX

Copyright © 2010 by William Maltese
Cover Graphic by Deana C. Jamroz

All rights reserved.
No part of this book may be reproduced in any form
without the expressed written consent
of the authors and publisher.
Printed in the United States of America

www.wildsidebooks.com

FIRST EDITION

CONTENTS

Dedication 8

Introduction 9

WARNING 13

TASTING FEES 17

WASHINGTON GRAPES 18

SPOKANE, WASHINGTON 20

Spokane Area Wineries 23

Arbor Crest Wine Cellars 24
Barili Cellars 31
Barrister Winery 35
Caterina Winery 41
Grande Ronde Cellars (+ Emvy Cellars, Masset
    Winery, Morrison Lane) 45
Knipprath Cellars 51
Latah Creek Wine Cellars 56

Liberty Lake Cellars 62
Lone Canary Winery 66
Mountain Dome Winery 72
Nodland Cellars 77
Overbluff Cellars 84
Robert Karl Cellars 89
Vintage Hill Cellars 95
Whitestone Winery 97

COLBERT AND MEAD (GREENBLUFF),
    WASHINGTON 103

Colbert and Mead (Greenbluff) Wineries 105
Terranova Cellars 106
Townshend Cellar 109
Trezzi Wine 114

THE PALOUSE AREA, WASHINGTON 121

PULLMAN, WASHINGTON 123

Pullman Wineries 125

Merry Cellars 126
Wawawai Canyon Winery 132

CLARKSTON, WASHINGTON 137

Clarkston Winery 139

Basalt Cellars 140
OTHER OPINIONS 144

Index 145

About the Author 147

DEDICATION

To

BONNIE CLARK,
Who came along for the tastings;

BRUCE CLARK,
Who was the "designated driver";

and

MICHAEL BURGESS,
Whose genius makes
THE TRAVELING GOURMAND SERIES
possible.

INTRODUCTION

I WAS BORN AND RAISED in Spokane, Washington. I went to Pratt Elementary School, Libby Junior High School, Lewis and Clark High School. I attended Washington State University in Pullman, Washington. After my graduation from the latter, I jettisoned the Spokane/Pullman area, like just about everyone else who has ever been born and raised there, to head off to places a little less quiet, a little less conservative…a lot more exotic, erotic, more culturally sophisticated, and a lot more "with it." Literally, I circled the globe a couple of times, often finding myself sipping the local wines in the vineyards of France, Germany, Italy, Spain, Chile, South Africa, and Australia….

Actually, my interest in wine occurred before I left the Pacific Northwest. My final university paper in Marketing/Advertising was based upon "The U.S. Pacific Coast. Wine Industry." However, at the time, there was no wine production in Washington State. There was none in Oregon State. Its emerging presence in California, on which I based my treatise, wasn't yet so far along that any of that state's wines were yet recognized as serious competition to its European counterparts.

My earliest ongoing long-term relationship with wine, therefore, was with those bottled by the long-established French châteaux; not so expensive, at the time that they couldn't be far more easily, monetarily, accessed and enjoyed than they are today. Imbibing Château Lafite-Rothschild, Château Margaux, Château Latour, Château Haut-Brion, Château Mouton-Rothschild, and Château D'Yquem, on the very ancient sites from which their grapes are still grown and harvested, spoiled me for years into thinking that the only really great wines were French wines. That early and long-lasting impression remained with me even as I and my nose and palate ventured farther afield with on-site sampling of German Spätburgunder, Muskattrollinger; Italian Valpolicella, Lambrusco, even Frascati whose history goes back 2,000 years to ancient Rome; Spanish Divus, Muruve Crianza; Chilean Cabernet Sauvignon; South African Pinotage and Bordeaux Blend Stellenbosch....

If my early awareness of the California wine industry kept me abreast of its burgeoning progress to the point where I eventually came around to admitting some of its product finally began seriously to compete with its European counterparts, I was actually surprised when I attended a dinner party at which my host produced a bottle of genuinely decent 2006 Winemaker's Reserve Pinot Noir from the Amity Vineyards in...of all places... Oregon. Even as I was packing my bags to head back to Spokane, after decades away, to hook up with my cousin, Bonnie Clark, with whom I'd been contracted by my publisher Wildside/Borgo Press to co-author *BACK OF THE BOAT GOURMET COOKING*, I kept in the back of my mind a determination to check more fully into what had been happening in Oregon since last I'd checked in there, several decades before, as regards winemaking.

However, if you ever wanted to see my face register surprise, I suspect you should have seen it when Bonnie, with several recipes of our co-authored book collaboration under our belts, wondered aloud if I'd like to consider recommending some local Washington wines to supplement our dishes.

Washington wines?

After a couple of weekends of visiting local tasting rooms with Bonnie and her husband, Bruce, the latter having graciously volunteered as "the designated driver," during which I finally found (at first I didn't think it was ever going to happen), a few Washington wines that actually weren't all that bad, I sent off a query to my publisher, wondering if Wildside/Borgo figured there were enough other wine fans out there, just as ignorant as I was as regarded Washington State's wine production, who might be interested in reading *WILLIAM MALTESE'S WINE TASTER'S DIARY: WASHINGTON STATE* as the first in the series of wine books I'd long-contemplated doing. I went to contract within the week; although my soon-discovered realization that there was actually a whole plethora of wineries blossomed in the state, since last I'd paid any attention, soon had the contract expanded to include three Washington *WINE TASTER'S* books (Eastern, Central, and Western Washington), and then expanded, yet again, to include a book for each of the presently existing eight Washington State wine-producing regions.

Therefore, be as surprised as I was, or not, to discover what Washington State has to offer, and/or doesn't, by way of wines for today's discerning, and/or not so discerning, wine-lover. To be followed up by seven other *WILLIAM MALTESE'S WINE TASTER'S DIARY* Washington books.

Also, already contracted for this series—*WILLIAM MALTESE'S WINE TASTER'S DAIRY: OKLAHOMA* by Rie McGaha and *WILLIAM MALTESE'S WINE TASTER'S DIARY: IN SEARCH OF OZ'S PERFECT PINOT (MORNINGTON PENINSULA)* by A. B. Gayle.

Bottom's up! Skoal! Prost! Cheers! Jambo! Salud! Gëzuar! Fisehatak! Genatzt! Gayola! Afiyæt oslun!...*et al.*

WARNING

NOT TO COME OFF sounding like a wine snob, but....

For anyone who has been drinking wine for a good many years and has developed a sophistication that appreciates the nuances of complex "nose" and complex "palate," don't come to Washington State, especially the Spokane/Pullman Wine Region, and expect to find any abundance of break-out wines to make your day, because it simply isn't going to happen—not for a good many more years anyway.

Washington commercial vineyards haven't been in existence long enough, and their winemakers haven't been making wine long enough, to produce any truly great wines, hampered, too, by a Washington State wine drinker who hasn't been drinking wine, Washington-State or otherwise, long enough for his nose and palate to have graduated beyond an appreciation of all wines "fruity" and, for whatever his reason (I suspect a climate that doesn't have all that many genuinely hot days), all wines red.

Local Spokane blogger, "Sip of Spokane," suggested to me that the latter was merely a case of the Washington-wine consumers having tried whites, developed a sophisticated palate, and moved on to the reds. Duh! Somehow, I don't think so, even though Bonnie argues that she started out on whites, just couldn't find one she liked, so moved on to the reds which suit her better; Bruce argues that "all" whites leave him with a genuinely unpleasant aftertaste. I am happy to report, though, that by this book's end, they'd actually found at least a couple of white wines they're now enjoying regularly.

Maybe my definition of "sophisticated palate" differs from that of everyone else, in assuming, I guess, that its one that's able to appreciate a whole spectrum of wines, red and white, and sometimes, albeit rarely, those in-between; I admit to still looking upon rosés as decidedly half-assed, the vintner not really having decided whether to leave the grape skins on, or off, so having compromised with something in between.

Also, a Washingtonian wants his wine, now…not tomorrow, not next week, not next year, certainly not several years down the line. The sooner he sees the grapes gone from vineyard to barrel, to bottle, to table, to down-his-throat, the happier he is. While I was in the area, the going "thing" was the purchase of aerators, through which newly uncorked wine can be poured, to eliminate even the hour or so sometimes necessary to naturally air a red vintage, and to bypass any and all bother, whatsoever, in doing a decant; not that any Washington wine is likely to be found with sediments that require a decant, unless the wine is spoiled by improper storage. Beware, by the way, all through Washington, of dry-cork syndrome, in that there's a tendency here, in most stores, homes, even in the wineries (possibly because of quick turnover), to store bottles upright.

For a number of reasons—a need to please their undiscerning customers, or not sell their product…small production lines, for the most part, many with a yearly maximum capacity of only 500 cases…neither the time, the money, nor the space to leave wine too long in any barrel—almost all Spokane/Pullman Wine Region wineries, with only a few exceptions, seem intent upon giving the local drinker exactly what he wants. Then, again, it may be, too, that the winemakers who gravitate to this area are merely just as similarly inclined as their target audience, because I can't tell you how many times I have heard how many of these local winemakers expound upon how their sole purpose in life is the production of a product they personally enjoy…because of its…tah-dah!…"robust *full-fruitiness*, with as much elimination as possible of interfering background flavors, like oak and tannin."

And, as previously mentioned, if your passion is white wine, you're in for additional disappointment. I can pretty much count upon the fingers of one hand the number of Washingtonians I met who actually liked white wine. Even Latah Creek, which built its excellent reputation on its superb whites, has recently bowed under pressure from the dominating preference for reds in the local marketplace, and has proceeded with attempts to shift its emphasis, so far with little success, into the red spectrum. Wine lovers will be in for a great loss if and when Latah Creek white wine quality suffers from this local consumer-driven segue.

None of which says that taking a wine-tasting road-trip through Washington can't be fun, interesting, and enjoyable, in that no one needs to imbibe truly great wines 24/7. Sometimes, one merely wants something to drink that doesn't take too much thought beyond uncorking, filling up a glass, and swallowing it on down (plenty of those kinds of wine here). Besides which, it has long been my philosophy that if you don't taste all sorts of wines, from rot-gut, to the plonk, to the so-so, to the very best, you're not truly going to appreciate the very best (even of the Washington wines) when you do taste them.

Besides which, wine-tasting, is a subjective activity, the results of which depend upon a whole lot of factors, not least of which is a person's personal likes and dislikes, not to mention that the same labeled wine can taste slightly, or a whole lot differently, from year to year, from vintage to vintage, because of attending weather conditions during growing and even when the grapes are harvested. So, just because I dislike something, doesn't mean that everyone does or should dislike it. Same thing goes for a wine I like. The fun of wine is in taking the adventure it provides in finding what you personally prefer, and in sticking to your guns, as far as liking it, not surrendering to the opinions of people, like myself, who sometimes seem to make the whole wine "thing" far more mystical and "insider-only" than it really is.

TASTING FEES

NOTHING IS FREE! Granted, there was a time when I drove the whole length and breadth of California's Napa Valley, stopping at each and every winery along the way, imbibing the fermented juice of the grape, without being anything out of pocket or pocketbook, but such times are no more. Not in California. Not in Oregon. Certainly not in Washington where low production, usually a maximum of 500 cases, prohibits wineries, looking at their bottom lines, from giving away free booze to anyone possibly out merely for a cheap drunk.

So, at each Spokane/Pullman WA tasting room you visit, be prepared to pay an average of $5 a person for a selection of samplings that can run from five to considerably more wines.

By way of trade-off for your contribution of hard-earned bucks, you can expect to see $5 deducted from the price of any bottle of wine that you decide to purchase on-site and take with you.

WASHINGTON GRAPES

SURPRISINGLY TO ME, Washington State's first wine grapes were planted at Fort Vancouver, on the state's western seaboard, by the Hudson's Bay Company, as early as 1825. Settlers of French, German, and Italian descent carried cuttings with them into the rest of the state, vineyards established in eastern Washington's Walla Walla Valley area by 1860.

The rich volcanic soils of eastern Washington, its arid climate, and concentrated launch of large-scale irrigation in 1903, were ideal for the European varietal grapes that were planted in the Yakima and Columbia Valleys, with continued rapid expansions that accounted for the first annual Columbia River Valley Grape Carnival, in Kennewick, in 1910.

This early spurt of grape cultivation in the state, however, was curtailed by the enactment of Prohibition in 1920, which might have provided the impetus for home winemaking that allowed quick establishment of the first bonded winery in western-Washington's Puget Sound region almost as soon as the ban on alcoholic beverages ended; some forty-two wineries in the state by 1938.

It wasn't until the 1960s, however, that any substantial commercial-scale planting was initiated. In the 1970s, there was really significant expansion of the industry. Although, it's only been since the mid-1970s that wine making, for Washington State, has become a three-billion-dollar-plus industry whose product is now sold worldwide.

The Washington Wine Commission, a unified marketing and trade association, was formed in 1987, followed in 1999 by the Washington Wine Quality Alliance (WWQA) that established industry standards in winemaking and labeling, and saw Washington as the first U.S. state to have definite "reserve" wine standards.

SPOKANE, WASHINGTON

Spō·kăn'

ORIGINALLY KNOWN as Spokane Falls, the city is located in the northwestern United States in eastern Washington, and is the largest city in, and the county seat of, Spokane County. It's located on the Spokane River, some 110 miles (180 km) south of the Canadian border, and about twenty miles (thirty-two km) from the Washington-Idaho state borders.

European settlement, in conjunction with the westward expansion, began with Canadian David Thompson who in 1810 established the North West Company's trading-post, Spokane House, which became the center of the fur trade between the Rockies and Cascades mountain ranges.

By the late 1800s, the Spokane area was best known for its gold and silver mining, and it was considered one of the most productive ore-producing regions in North America. In 1871, the city officially incorporated, deriving its name, "Children of the Sun," from local Native American Salish. Major settlement began with the completion of the Northern Pacific Railroad in 1881.

Presently, Spokane, nicknamed "The Lilac City" because of the profusion of those flowers which have thrived here since their introduction in the twentieth century, is the second largest city in Washington, taking second seat only to Seattle on the state's west coast.

SPOKANE AREA WINERIES

ARBOR CREST WINE CELLARS
(est. 1982)

4705 N. Fruithill Rd.
Spokane, Washington 99217
Telephone: (509) 745-3903
eMail: info@arborcrest.com
Website: www.arborcrest.com

Tasting Room open daily 12-5 pm, extended summer hours.

NO ONE UNDER 21

From I-90, take Argonne Exit (287).

Go north on Argonne.

Cross the Spokane River.

On Upriver Drive, turn right and go less than one mile.

Turn left, onto Fruithill Road.

Make a sharp right at the top of the hill into the winery's private drive.

Or

From Bigelow Gulch, take Lehman south.

Turn left onto Fruithill Road.

* * * * * * *

YOU CAN SEE THIS WINERY, which receives over 60,000 visitors annually, from a long way away, perched atop a basalt cliff, above the Spokane River, peering out over the landscape of the valley below, and looking very much like a very impressive eagle's aerie.

My next impression, though, upon beginning the narrow and curvy, access road, and knowing that it would, likewise, have to be a road driven even more carefully on the way back, was confirmation of every warning I'd ever received NOT to drink and drive. Too many wine tastings at the top might very well result in not ever getting all of the way back down to the bottom (except possibly by stretcher). Someone had done just that the year before.

The winery's Cliff House, with four acres of gardens and seventy-five acres of surrounding grounds, as well as the view from its cliff-top position, is truly pleasing to the eye.

The house, a three-storied Florentine mansion and National Historic Landmark, was built in 1924 as residence for Royal Newton Riblet, and it was considered one of the most "electric" homes in the United States, at the time, complete with an electric fireplace and a built-in refrigerator. Riblet was the inventor and patent-holder for such devices as the pattern sprinkler system, mechanical parking garage, and the square-wheel tractor; one of the latter in display on the grounds. Riblet and his seventh wife, Mildred, lived in the house until he died in 1960, and she stayed on until her death in 1978. The most convenient access used to be a five-passenger tram (now gone), built in 1927 at the suggestion of Riblet's brother, Byron, who was a chairlift manufacturer. The tram arrived and departed a tram house, on the opposite side of the Spokane River, and carried visitors over the water and up the 450-foot cliff; fishing the river from the tram became a popular pastime for Riblet's houseguests.

Surrounds include an arched gatekeeper's house (later converted into guest quarters), sunken rose garden, open-air pagoda, terraced flower and herb gardens, a life-sized checkerboard, a 60,000-gallon pool fashioned from natural basalt from the adjoining cliffs but no longer used for swimming, a croquet court made out of cement that used to be covered in summer months with a layer of sand to prevent its balls from rolling too far afield, and covered in the winter with frozen water for use as a skating rink.

In 1984, the estate was purchased by brothers Harold and David Mielke, and Harold's wife Marcia. The Mielke family had farmed in Washington State for over a century and had discovered in the 1970s that its land had enormous potential by way of growing grapes for quality wine. Arbor Crest Wine Cellars was established in 1982 when the family-owned cherry orchards were downed, the land converted into vineyards; winery equipment, purchased from a belly-up California winery, was shipped directly to the old cherry-processing plant for producing the winery's first official vintage.

Sole ownerships of the Cliff House and Arbor Crest Wine Cellars, were transferred, in 1999, to Harold and Marcia who brought in their daughter Kristina Mielke-van Loben Sels, as chief winemaker, and their son-in-law, Jim, as someone with invaluable expertise in agricultural economics and viticulture. Kristina grew up helping with the family business and graduated University of California Davis with a degree in Fermentation Science. Her job as an enologist for Ferrari-Carano Vineyards and Winery just outside Healdsburg, California, saw her promoted to associate winemaker in 1997, in which capacity she served until joining her parents at Arbor Crest where she immediately converted white-wine making tanks into red-wine fermenters, and initiated other changes, to give the family business more options. While focusing on main varietals—Chardonnay, Sauvignon Blanc, Merlot, and Cabernet Sauvignon—Kristina is also producing Pinot Gris and Sirah.

Supplementing with grapes from the Columbia Valley, Red Mountain, and Wahluke Slopes, many bought from the same vineyards for decades, Arbor Crest is able to produce, and does, a wide variety of wines, red and white. The five varieties of grapes planted as the small five-acre Cliff House vineyard, grow in weather conditions cool enough, at that 2,500-feet-above-sea level elevation, to produce Arbor Crest's estate-bottled sparkling wine which isn't available for tasting. I was pleased the winery had the professional decency, though, to call its product "sparkling wine" instead of the inaccurate, outside of France—but often blatantly hijacked-by-Americans—"champagne."

Named one of the "Top 50 Producers Every Wine Lover Should Know," by *Wine Spectator*, Arbor Crest is best known for its Sauvignon Blanc and for its red "Dionysus," a blend of Cabernet Sauvignon, Merlot, and Cabernet Franc. In a blind-tasting test of nearly 100 Northwest chardonnays, conducted by *Wine Press Northwest*, the winery's Columbia Valley and Conner Lee Vineyard finished with coveted "Outstanding" ratings.

Although the present tasting room at the Cliff House wasn't built until 2003, it architecturally blends in perfectly within its older environment, and is often booked for weddings and other special events because of its location and charm. Likewise, at least during my visit, it lived up to its reputation of having a staff well-versed in the nuances of the company's products. At least I can say that for Nerissa, who provided my tasting of five Arbor Crest wines, after my payment of the required five-dollar-tasting fee, and who was quick to point out—in response to my complaint that so few Washington wines seemed, unlike French wines, to need or get any aging before drinking— that the Petite Sirah (Wahluke Slope Vineyard) I'd just tasted had been bottled four years previously, and the Cabernet Sauvignon (Stillwater Creek Vineyard) three years before. She was just as quickly eager to point out to me that the Arbor Crest wines just kept getting better and better as the vines from which their grapes were picked kept getting older and older—some of those vines as much as—gasp!—thirty years old. While I didn't have the heart to comment upon the grand old age of some vineyards in France, even some vines in California boasting over a hundred candles on their birthday cakes, thirty years *is* an old vine for Washington State. While the state can boast grapes growing within its boundaries as far back as the end of the nineteenth century, those were either all uprooted, and replaced by orchards, during Prohibition, or flooded out by the reservoir formed behind the Grand Coulee Dam.

Despite Nerissa's cheerleading on behalf of Washington State reds, and the Arbor Crest's winemaker's best ongoing attempts, I found the Arbor Crest reds pretty much as thin as most of their peers from competing Washington State wineries. More and more, I'm gravitating toward Washington State whites, some of which I've found truly exceptional. I particularly enjoyed the Arbor Crest Riesling (Dionysus Vineyard) and its Sauvignon Blanc (Bacchus Vineyard). I went so far as to recommend to my co-author of *BACK OF THE BOAT GOURMET COOKING*, Bonnie Clark, who was with me, in our search of a few good Washington State wines to accompany the recipes in our book, that the Arbor Crest Chardonnay (Columbia Valley), what with its buttery toasted oak flavor, and its subtle apple-and-spice highlights, might genuinely go well with one of our grilled fish or chicken recipes. She concurred, after which I purchased a bottle of each mentioned wine, as well as a bottle of Arbor Crest "Sparkling Wine," all for later, and we successfully made it down the mountain. *Hallelujah! Hosanna! Gloria in excelsis Deo.*

The bottle of sparkling wine, by the way, turned out to be so-so, but was saved by the addition of Xoçai® Xe®, the energy drink (a "Xomosa"), which often helps me get through so-so bottles of sparkling wine and so-so bottles of champagne—even France not coming through with bubbly perfection one-hundred percent of the time.

****

In our book *BACK OF THE BOAT GOURMET COOKING*, Bonnie and I recommended the following Arbor Crest wine to go with:

Oysters
Arbor Crest Wine Cellars "Sparkling Wine"

NOTE: For anyone unable to make the drive to Arbor Crest's Hill House, the winery does offer its attractive tasting room in downtown Spokane, right off Riverside Park. It's an atmospheric little niche, complete with tasting bar, tables, chairs, dim-lighting, in an otherwise modern shopping mall. The day I was there, the tastings were the very same as those available at the Hill House tasting room, and the bottle of Arbor Crest "Sparkling Wine" I purchased was conveniently chilled for immediate drinking.

2nd Tasting Room in Spokane's River Park Square

808 W. Main Ave 3rd Floor, Next to AMC ticket both
Spokane WA 99201
Telephone # (509) 747-3903

Open daily, with extended summer hours.

BARILI CELLARS
(est. 2009)

608 West 2nd Avenue
Spokane, Washington 99201
Telephone: (509) 995-4077 or (509) 979-5830
eMail: info@barillicellars.com
Website: www.barillicellars.com

Tasting Room hours available upon query
NO ONE UNDER 21

APPARENTLY, GETTING ACCESS to Barili Cellars cellar, and/or its tasting room, let alone getting any tastes of its wines, is decidedly difficult to do. That I didn't have to wait all that long had nothing to do with my involvement, at the time, in writing not one but two books—this one, and my *BACK OF THE BOAT GOURMET COOKING* with Bonnie Clark—which required my researching Washington State wines. Nor had it anything to do with Barili Cellars only producing genuinely stellar wines that always have a long list of wine connoisseurs waiting to grab it up; neither of which is true.

It had everything to do with the winery's extremely limited production (with a proposed leveling out at a maximum of 500 cases), and with its owners' admission that their wide circle of family and friends, combined with Spokane's yearly wine-tasting marathon, held each Mother's Day weekend by all local wineries (that sees a couple thousand people through tasting-room doors), usually sees Barili's small production gone before summer even sets in. Finally, it had to do with my arrival in Spokane just happening to coincide with the Cellars' release party for its four latest wines—a Viognier, a Chardonnay (with thirty days of barrel-fermentation), a "Barrelin' Red" (a blend of Syrah, Cabernet Sauvignon, and Merlot), and a Cabernet Sauvignon; the reds having spent sixteen months in American/Hungarian oak barrels (future plans entail a shift to oak barrels even more tightly grained).

Barili Cellars is the collaboration between Russ Feist and Steve Trabun. Both men worked for the same employer, Avista Power, and were, likewise, independent home winemakers, on the side, producing very small outputs of fruit wines, when, in 2005, Russ had a scheduling conflict which made it impossible for him to pick up grapes from his source located in Prosser, Washington. Steve volunteered to do the deed, his grape source one and the same, and the idea for Barili Cellars began its initial germination, then and there, nurtured by Steve's wife, Dana, having graduated the enology program at nearby Washington State University.

With an assist from a local businessman, Steve Salvatori, space in an entrepreneurial center for start-up businesses was provided and transformed into both tasting room and winery-production facility. Both areas, by the way, the latter in the "basement," are exceedingly clean and crisp and pleasing to the eye. The tasting room is especially cheery with its brightly painted walls, with its color-coordinated artwork, its service bar, and its Barili logo prominently displayed in its large front window.

The afternoon we were there for tasting, there were several other people out to advantage the rare access occasion. The atmosphere was friendly and convivial. The two admittedly charming and friendly vintners each wearing black t-shirts with WE WORK FOR WINE across the back, were readily located within the crowd, allowing one and all to know exactly in which direction to head when glasses were empty and in need of refills. Likewise, Dana was behind the bar, at the rear, providing immediate assistance for anyone wanting to buy a bottle to go.

In the end, while I bought a bottle of the Barili Viognier (a Washington State white winning my day, again) to take home for more leisurely (and, as it turned out, okay) exploration, I passed on the Chardonnay, as well as on both supposed stars of the day, the "Barrelin' Red" and the Cabernet Sauvignon. The reds just didn't come across full-bodied enough for my taste. While I thought the Cabernet just might please the palate of Bonnie, she complained that the wine's chocolate and raspberry undertones, with its lingering spiciness (whoa!!!), just wasn't the kind of pencil-shaving taste-experience for which she was always looking.

In fact, anyone who has a preference for the slight pucker of tannin on the taste buds, is apt to be decidedly disappointed, for a long time to come, by the production from Barili whose owners readily confess to their personal preference for "fruity, not oaken," that has them continuing in a conscious effort to achieve the former, to the detriment of the latter.

Also, I have to confess to an inherent bias I have against any winery that is a winery merely as a sideline for its owners who have regular day jobs. There's just something about my buying wine, produced by way of hobby, even knowing as I do how genuinely more adamant some people can be about their hobbies, enjoyed, than about their regular jobs, not enjoyed, that leads me to suspect that I'm not getting the kind of quality product I would be getting if attention had been devoted 24/7 to the winemaking.

****

In our book *BACK OF THE BOAT GOURMET COOKING*, Bonnie and I recommended the following Barili Cellars wine to go with:

Salmon cakes
Barili Cellars "Barrelin' Red"

BARRISTER WINERY
(est. 2001)

1213 Railroad Avenue
Spokane, Washington 99201
Telephone: (509) 465-3591
eMail: barristerwinery@aol.com
Website: www.barristerwinery.com

Tasting Room open daily 12-6 pm, Friday; 12-5, Saturday. NO ONE UNDER 21

This winery is really hard to find but well worth the finding.

Drive west on Second Avenue to Jefferson (about 12 blocks west of Division Street).

Turn right on Jefferson.

Turn left on Railroad Avenue (immediately before going under the railroad viaduct). NOTE: Railroad Avenue is on the south side of the railroad overpass; Railroad Alley is on the north side; which can become a bit confusing).

NOTE: If you still find you're having problems, give them a call.

DESPITE THE FACT THAT, as far as its exterior, Barrister's premises, in a 100-year-old brick building in the historic Davenport Arts District, in downtown Spokane, don't compare to the panoramic vistas afforded by Arbor Crest, from the latter's lofty cliff top, or with the enchanting Spanish-mission architecture of Latah Creek, Barrister's interior has to be the finest by way of any Spokane wine-tasting facility with its large and dimly-lit atmospheric space, complete with fourteen-foot high brick walls, and filled with wine, wine bar, wine barrels, attentive staff (Judi and Betty the day we were there), and the "Barrel Room," the latter for wedding receptions, rehearsal dinners, corporate board dinners, Christmas and holiday parties coordinated and catered by Beacon Hill Events and Catering.

The very fact that Barrister is so hard to find makes the satisfaction in finding it the same as for someone who's a private club member and one of the few with access to clubhouse facilities.

Your arrival is tastefully confirmed by the Barrister logo (purple grape clusters balanced on mirroring sides of a golden scales) emblazoned on a wine barrel lid, suspended above the huge wooden entrance doors. The cement of the access ramp is attractively decorated with intaglio grape-and grape-leaf designs that likewise clue you into the treat in store inside.

As the name of the winery, "Barristers" implies, it was founded by two attorneys-at-law, Greg Lipsker and Michael White, in a laundry room, and with a five-gallon Zinfandel home-winemaking kit the two purchased in 1997, as a whim, while their two families were on vacation in British Columbia. They'd just stopped in at a shop to buy a couple of bottles of wine and discovered all of the tools needed for winemaking, on their own; all of which resulted in their first vintage served up to friends.

They entered four of their wines in the Indy International amateur wine competition and came away with three gold and one silver medal, which made them have a "Sally Field moment" and think, maybe, people "really do like" our wines.

By 2000, they were processing one and one-half tons of grapes in Greg's garage and soon expanded into a 1,500-square-foot basement location near the Spokane Arena.

By 2001, their hobby had expanded to where they took the major jump to fully bonded winery, their new and larger facility on Railroad Avenue, and the shedding of their law careers to become full-time winemakers.

Initially only into red-wine production, the two have since ventured into occasional small quantities of white, but reds remain their specialty (their Cabernet Franc having a cult-like following), with hand-picked grapes incoming from several of Washington State's most well-known vineyards—Pepper Bridge and Klipsum (and from a couple not-so-well-known—Dwelley and Artz), fermentation (via eleven different strains) taking place in small lots, barreled in French oak (from four different forests) and American oak, for from sixteen to forty months.

They've gleaned "Best of Show" at the Wines of the World, the Northwest Wine Summit, the Tri-Cities Wine Festival, as well as pulled in the prestigious "Platinum" from *Wine Press Northwest.*

When we were there, they were introducing four new wines:

Riesling, from old vines at the Koinonia Vineyard near Sunnyside

Cabernet Sauvignon, Sagemoor

Sangiovese, Kiona Vineyard on Red Mountain

Merlot, Walla Walla Valley

And offered tastings of their—

"Rough Justice" (a blend of Merlot, Syrah, Cabernet Franc, and Cabernet Sauvignon)

Also, usually only available to the Barrister Wine Club Members (via a $90 fee, paid twice a year for three pre-selected bottles of wine, each time), we sampled their limited releases of excellent....

Cabernet Sauvignon, Red Mountain (a bottle of which I ended up buying).

Cabernet Sauvignon, Pepper Bridge.

Like most Washington State wineries, Barrister is driven by the taste preference of its customers and by the personal self-confessed preference of its winemakers, and is, therefore, intent upon gearing its total production toward "fruit-flavored, soft-tannin (no-bite) wines, with really long and silky finishes." While I realize the intense capital and space investment required for the production of higher tannin-content European-style wines that require longer aging, I do wish, somewhere along the line, winemakers, like Mike and Greg, would somehow find it within their means to venture into wines with tad more sophisticated nose and palate than fruity…fruity…always predominately fruity.

For those of us "into" art, as well as wine, Barrister Winery, on the first Friday of every month, hangs the artwork of some local artist. The artist is there in person between five and seven P.M. After which, there's usually acoustical blues played by "Lonesome" Lyle Morse. Beacon Hill Events and Catering provides its for-sale buffet of bistro-style food which can be enjoyed with a purchase of Barrister Wine by the glass or by the bottle.

Occasionally, too, you can hook up with the winery for one of its barge trips through the French countryside. Since Bonnie and Bruce had been on the brink of joining the last one, we spent several minutes chatting up Barrister co-owner Mike Lipsker, and learning what they'd missed, as well as trying to persuade Barrister to host yet another adventure into great French wines, cuisine, and canal-latticed countryside.

****

In our book *BACK OF THE BOAT GOURMET COOKING*, Bonnie and I recommended the following Barrister Winery wine to go with:

…Steaks with Spice Rub
Barrister Winery "Rough Justice"

Buffalo and Beef Burgers
Barrister Winery Cabernet Franc

Brian's Hot Wings
Barrister Winery Riesling

CATERINA WINERY
(est. 1993)

Located in the historical Broadview Dairy Building
905 N. Washington
Spokane, Washington 99201
Telephone: (509) 328-5069
eMail: info@caterina.com
Website: www.caterinawinery.com

Tasting Room open Wednesday-Sunday, 12-6 P.M.
NO ONE UNDER 21

ALTHOUGH THIS WINERY BOASTS boutique wines, like its Willard Family vineyard Cabernet Sauvignon, and its Viognier, which rated, respectively, ninety-two and ninety-one points from *Wine Spectator* magazine, I confess to not being impressed in the least with what I tasted during its much ballyhooed Grand Opening under new ownership.

Founded by winemaker Mike Scott, Spokane pioneer winemaker (now of Lone Canary—a winery which might well have gone belly-up by the time this book reaches publication), it almost closed its doors in 2009, the result—or so go the rumors—of a conflict of interest occurring when it couldn't decide whether or not it was a venue for wine or for beer and live music. Whatever its difficulties, it was rescued from extinction by Don Townshend, owner of Spokane's Townshend Cellar. Don has a long history with Caterina, having honed his early wine-making skills there, and that inclined him to believe it warranted his efforts to save it.

So, while Townshend Cellar and Caterina now share the same wine-making facility, Don professes a commitment to different styles for each company; Caterina aimed entirely toward production of main-stream new-world wines with less oak-time and fruit-forward flavors (sorry Bonnie!), all for less than $20 a bottle.

Our visit to the renovated Caterina tasting room had Bonnie comment that it was, as advertised, less broken up and confining than it was on her last visit. The space does have a lot to offer, as does its open-air patio that fronts (albeit from a great distance) Spokane's attractive Riverside Park. The new layout, though, in my opinion, was all the Grand Opening had to boast. The wine served up was so undistinguishable and mediocre that I tossed much of it, as well as my wine-tasting menu and score card, at the end of my visit, figuring none of it warranted comment.

My problem, I suspect, derived from how the Grand Opening ballyhooed Townshend's arrival as the new owner, ushering in a new era of Caterina wines, leading at least me to expect something different from the plonk that put Caterina in its decline. When in fact, what was offered up for tasting was the same old product that put Caterina in its tail-spin.

Now, I have nothing whatsoever against Townshend having served up old product as part of his winery's new beginning, had it been made perfectly apparent from the get-go that what we would be drinking was inventory left over from before. In fact, that would have been a genuinely legitimate way for him to not only get rid of some of the old stuff but provide opportunity for those who did like it and wanted to buy some. However, for anyone who came expecting a resurrected superb product from a resurrected once-superb winery, aside from renovation of architectural features of its surround, disappointment was likely pre-destined before we ever stepped through the Caterina door.

Maybe in a few years, when Townshend has had time to make the wines his, and his, alone, I'll try them again. Then, again, what with so many wines available in Washington State, maybe I won't.

* * * * * * *

NOTE: A little farther on, during the course of my tour of this region, we stopped off at the Townshend Cellar tasting room and remarked upon how good some of those wines were in comparison to the genuinely disappointing Caterina wines we experienced at the Caterina Grand Opening that announced Don Townshend's takeover and assumption of control of these facilities. Graciously, Jill Rider, the gal serving up the wine samples from behind the Townshend Cellar bar told us that any time we'd like to schedule another stop-by of the Caterina tasting room, she'd be more than happy to make arrangements to be there, personally, to hopefully provide us a better time than our first go-round.

In the end, I refused Jill's kind offer for any such second visit, because I didn't think that it, under those individualized special circumstances, would truly reflect the same experience likely to be had by any reader of this book, not an author of a book on the wines of the region, if and when you drop in at Caterina's, unannounced.

A guide representative of the special treatment that can often be had by VIPs, and often is, is, I think, best left to another, separate, volume.

GRANDE RONDE CELLARS
(est. 1997)

Located in the historical Broadview Dairy Building
906 W. Second Avenue
Spokane, Washington 99201
Telephone: (509) 455-8161
eMail: dave@granderondecellars.com
Website: www.granderondecellars.com

(A "cooperative wine-tasting venue" that includes not only the wines of Grande Ronde Cellars, but sometimes the wines of other wineries, like Mountain Dome; although tastings of all but Grande Ronde wine aren't always available).

Tasting Room hours Saturday 12-6 P.M.
NO ONE UNDER 21

Our first visit:

AND HERE'S YET ANOTHER Spokane wine-tasting facility (See Arbor Crest Wine Cellars and Liberty Lake Wine Cellars) with an access…its wide and very long, albeit straight-descent stairway…that encourages all tasters to arrive sober and leave the same way. Bonnie, who suffers from vertigo, required me to walk the stairway directly in front of her, at least on her way down.

Upon reaching the bottom of the stairs, however, you're in for a genuine treat, as regards the illusion that you've pretty much entered a below-ground wine-storage catacomb. There's dim-lighting, bottles of wine, barrels of wine, a bar set-up for serving wine, local artwork on the walls, and a separately licensed area, complete with tables and chairs, for small conventions, private parties, and wedding receptions. There's a wide selection of wine-related gifts, including wine-motif vases, baskets, even hand-carved gnomes. The first Friday of every month is devoted to combining wine tasting with the promotion of local artists and their work. There are regularly held wine-awareness and wine-food pairing classes. Flyers for an upcoming "Painting With Spirits" advertised opportunities "to create your own masterpieces during a three-hour creative session, conducted by local artist Cindi Schneider, who provides the subject for the session and works right along side the group, offering step-by-step guidance, everything—canvas, paint brushes, easel, and paint palate—included."

I counted some forty-one wines available from the purchase list, fifteen of those from Grande Ronde, the other from four other Washington wineries (Mountain Dome, Emvy Cellars, Masset Winery, and Morrison Lane) that Grande Ronde owner, David Westfall, brought together for this collective wine-tasting facility. Be forewarned, however, that you're not likely to get to sample any of the wines, other than Grande Ronde product, except, once or twice during any year, when those particular wineries are showcased; with the exception of Mountain Dome whose non-vintage sparkling wine was offered up the day we were there. Since Grande Ronde wines are produced at the same facility as Mountain Dome, there's kind of an incestuous relationship between those two wineries.

We sampled the Grande Ronde "Kibitzer Convention" (Riesling), "Cellar White" (Sauvignon Blanc, Sémillon), non-vintage Chardonnay, and its "Bridge Press" Merlot. That selection was more than adequate, considering the flight of stairs we were required to mount at the finish of our sipping session.

Did I mention that Grande Ronde Cellars focuses its production on—ta-dah!—red wines? Seven Hills Vineyard, and Pepper Bridge Vineyard, the sources of many of the winery's grapes, are considered the cornerstones of Grande Ronde's successful reds. Although receiving assurances that its "Cellar Red" was rife with "tobacco-scented black cherry and currant," Bonnie and I agreed that it predominantly tasted disconcertingly of dill.

While Bonnie and Bruce pooh-poohed the "Cellar White," I found it, as advertised—refreshingly bright and crisp and something I'd be more than happy to serve chilled with a turkey sandwich. And I appreciated Grande Ronde's willingness to let its Chardonnay age on its lees in 100% French oak barrels, followed by two months in stainless steel tanks, before bottling, although the non-vintage Chardonnay served up the day we were there was a little too "buttery" for even my palate; Bruce and Bonnie didn't bother finishing theirs.

In the end, I took home a bottle of untasted "Kibitzer Transfer" (Black Muscat) that when tasted, later, proved to be adequately sweet, and a nice complement for the chicken with which I ate it.

The history of Grande Ronde Cellars is uniquely that of one man, David Westfall, whose unsuccessful attempts to bring good wines to the Spokane area—in his capacity, firstly, as caterer…secondly, as retail wine-shop owner… finally, as wholesale wine distributor—finally saw him turn, in frustration, to his own wherewithal to turn quality grapes into his own product, in partnership with John Mueller and David Page, as Grande Ronde Cellars.

* * * * * * *

In our book *BACK OF THE BOAT GOURMET COOKING*, Bonnie and I recommended the following Grande Ronde Cellars wine to go with:

…Inside-Out Bleu-Cheese Buffalo Burger
Grande Ronde Cellars "Cellar Red"

…Rib-eye Steak
Grande Ronde Cellars "Charlotte's Cuvee"

MY SECOND VISIT:

I RETURNED to the Ronde Cellars tasting room, because I was trying to decide whether or not to include three of the cooperative's wineries (Emvy Cellars, Masset Winery, and Morrison Lane) in this book, and I needed some clarification. Admittedly, all three wineries had a token presence in Spokane, but their wines merely listed on the Grande Ronde tasting menu seemed really too little to merit any real attention, especially since the Masset Winery is headquartered in Wapato, Washington, and Morrison Lane is physically in Walla Walla, Washington—both locations out of the Spokane/Pullman Washington wine region and more likely included in some other book of my series—*WALLA WALLA VALLEY, WA WINES* and *YAKIMA VALLEY & RATTLESNAKE HILLS, WA WINES*. It seemed to me that all three wineries used the Grande Ronde tasting room as a retail outlet, like a grocery store, more than as a bona-fide tasting-room. If neither I, nor any other John D. Public, could show up at Grande Ronde and expect a sample of the Emvy, Masset, and Morrison products, I figured the trio pretty much deserved a bypass.

The afternoon of my return, a bottle of Masset Winery's Cabernet Sauvignon and a bottle Emvy Cellar's "Devotion" had just been opened.

I wasn't impressed by the Cabernet Sauvignon, and, with no chance of tasting any of the other nine listed Masset Winery wines, I've decided to exclude that winery from any individual listing in this book, as well as Morrison Lane; the latter never did, in my presence, have any of its bottles opened at the Grande Ronde tasting room. Possibly, I'll include them whenever my continuing series has expanded to include their official home bases (Wapato and Walla Walla).

In the end, I'm not prepared to give Emvy Winery more than I footnote, either, since it only has one wine to its credit, and I found its "Devotion" (special blend with fruit sourced from the famous Seven Hills Vineyard) nothing to write home (or write here) about. However, since Grande Ronde does seem to be its one and only mailing address, all of its bottling done by Grande Ronde (meaning, by Mountain Dome)...and since there's a rare chance you might get a taste, on a stop-by at Grande Ronde...just know that....

Mark and Valerie (MV) created Emvy CELLARS as a result of their wine hobby, and they did so with the help of Dave Westfall and John Mueller of Grande Ronde.

Telephone: (509) 995-2697
eMail: unavailable at time of printing
Website: www.emvycellars.com/index.html

KNIPPRATH CELLARS
(est. 1991)

5634 E. Commerce
Spokane, Washington 99212
Telephone: (509) 534-5121
eMail: grapesoknipprath@aol.com
Website: www.knipprath-cellars.com

Tasting Room open Wed-Sun 12-5 P.M.
NO ONE UNDER 21

From I-90, take Sprague Avenue exit.

Travel west to Fancher (just west of freeway overpass).

Turn north onto Fancher.

Drive to Commerce (second left, past Trent).

Winery is brick building on left (the old Parkwater Schoolhouse).

DO NOT MISS this winery if you're an aficionado of extremely good port; Knipprath (pronounced "Nip-Wrath")

Cellars has a genuinely well-deserved international award-winning reputation for its ports/dessert wines.

Even if you're not a fan of port or dessert wines, this winery, under its La Bodega del Norte branding (new, different, and not-liked-by-many label), provides an excellent white—"Marisa Roussane / Albariño," an unusual-to-be sure "Rosa" (not a *rosé*, not a *blush*, mind you), and a trio of good-tasting reds—"Elaine Vino Tinto," "K Sera Syrah," and Tempranillo…not to overlook its bottled sangría, "Milagro Sangría de Columbia," that rivals anything I've ever tasted during any of my many trips through Mexico where sangría takes pride of place at many a fiesta.

All Knipprath ports/dessert wines (red and white), and more traditional wines (red and white), were served up, the afternoon we were there (and we stayed for three full hours, having such a good time of it), by the winemaker's absolutely charming and knowledgeable mother, Christa, who, originally from Germany, then California, came north to give her son and winemaker, Henning Knipprath, a helping hand, "for a few weeks," and ended up staying on for the duration. And believe me when I say that the ambience of the tasting room would be missing a helluva lot without her there. The lady exudes old-world charm, elegance, graciousness, good humor, and a genuine comprehension of the winery's product.

Henning developed his initial interest in wine and viniculture in Germany, later in California, transitioning from a career as a military pilot; a career move he often, in the beginning, came to question, in the face of his having sacrificed a recession-proof job, with good retirement and medical benefits, for the often more mercurial life-style of a Spokane winemaker. Luckily, his ability to create wines with a European flair, employing methods of wine-making traditionally employed in the various wine regions of Europe, have paid off for him in the end, as Bonnie, Bruce, and I can verify. And, of course, his exceptional reputation for ports and dessert wines has made Knipprath Cellars world-renowned.

Speaking of those ports/dessert wines:

"Pink"—a Grenache/Syrah blend, with pinkish hue, which Bonnie and I can't wait to pair with strawberry cheese cake; the label's distinctive neon-red ribbon graphic indicating how a percentage of the proceeds from each bottle sold goes toward the prevention of breast cancer.

"Lagrima"—a white port that Christa went the extra mile to serve up to us "the traditional way," poured over a small bit of slightly squeezed lemon, then cooled down slightly by the addition of a frozen grape; a larger "Spritzer" version only needing a taller glass, more ice, and some tonic or soda.

"Matrix Port"—crafted from Washington State Syrah had us all anxious to have it with one of Bonnie and my *BACK OF THE BOAT GOURMET COOKING* grilled meats (rib-eye!).

"NV Positron Port"—award wining and aged in French and Spanish oak.

"Coffee Port"—so popular with customers that it was all sold out.

"LaV!" Dessert Wine—wondrously tasting of vanilla beans imported from Madagascar and Mexico.

"Au Chocolat!" (that's an exclamation point, at the end, by the way, not the "l" that Bonnie always assumed and constantly had her mispronouncing)—a blend of Columbia Valley reds, chocolate extracts, and grape spirits, for a truly marvelous dessert-wine drinking experience.

****

In our book *BACK OF THE BOAT GOURMET COOKING*, Bonnie and I recommended the following Knipprath Cellars wine to go with:

… relaxing and watching a beautiful sunset.
Knipprath Cellar's chocolate-flavored port-style "Au Chocolat!"….

NOTE: Christa provided us with one of her "Special Blend Cocktail" treats made from two-thirds "Au Chocolat!," one-third vanilla "LaV!," and a frozen grape (red or white does nicely).

Christa only smiles at how many times she has had people call in to order the delicious "vanilla/chocolate port" that doesn't exist, rather requires some bartending skills, instead.

NOTE: Christa, encyclopedia of information that she is, recommended that I remind my readers that port is a wine that, if kept away from hot places, only gets better the longer its bottle is opened. In fact, it's ongoing procedure in Europe to sometimes open a bottle and leave it for as long as a month before taking the first sip of the contents.

Christa recently found an open bottle of their "La V!" which had gone undetected for two years that ended up providing her and some lucky tasters (alas, not I!) with truly exceptional drinking experiences.

LATAH CREEK WINE CELLARS (est. 1982)

13030 E Indiana Ave
Spokane, Washington 99216
Telephone: (509) 926-0164
eMail: info@latahcreek.com
Website: www.latahcreek.com

Tasting Room open daily 9-5.
NO ONE UNDER 21

From I-90, take Pines Road Exit (289).

Go north to Indiana (the first traffic light).

Turn right on Indiana.

Proceed east for two blocks.

THERE'S A REASON this winery, in my opinion, is heads above all others in the Spokane area, even topping the visually impressive Arbor Crest. Not just because Latah Creek Wine Cellars was heralded by *Wine Spectator* magazine as one of the top producers of Merlot in the

State of Washington; although its Merlot is decidedly exceptional. Not just because its old-Spanish mission-style architecture, complete with bell-tower and tile walkways, is so eye-catching in its Washington State setting; one of the only small wineries in the state in a building specifically constructed to be a winery. Not just because of its extensive one-of-a-kind gift shop where Bonnie and I do all of our shopping for the likes of Roasted Garlic and Eggplant Spread for the recipes in our *BACK OF THE BOAT GOURMET COOKING*. Not just because of its large wine-tasting room and impressive tasting bar, the latter tended by a well-informed, polite, and helpful staff, including Penny and Christine who were behind the counter the afternoon we were there. Not just because the owners, Ellena and Mike Conway are so personable and friendly, Ellena's two recipe books, *JUST RELEASED* and *JUST RELEASED NO. 2* (her "Succulent Shredded Pork" is to die for!), musts for any serious cook. What makes it so special, at least in my book, is that it's one of the few wineries in this region that actually has a selection of white wines, all pretty damned good, and all so inexpensively priced that I usually feel guilty in having so often paid so much more for so much less. The superior quality of Latah Creek whites is attributed by Mike to a slow-cold fermentation process that brings out natural residual sweetness at lower alcohol levels.

In a landscape dotted with wineries whose winemakers seem to specialize in reds, maybe because most eastern Washingtonians, for some reason (maybe the long winters and cold climate for so much of the year), tend to bypass superlative whites in their stampede to chug-a-lug reds genuinely mediocre in comparison, I was truly overjoyed to find this unexpected cache of truly fine and inexpensive whites.

Mike and Ellena truly believe in giving their customers the best value for their wine bucks. As a result, their wines, red and white, all made from the same grapes found in the more expensive wines of their competition, sell for around only $10 a bottle. Is it any wonder, I couldn't help myself as far as carrying off a case?!

When we were there, the Latah Creek Wine List included eight whites and blushes, dry to sweet: Chardonnay, Sémillon, Riesling (my particular favorite), a "Huckleberry d'Latah" (not high on my list, if only because if I want to taste huckleberries, I prefer eating the berries), "Spokane Blush," Muscat Canelli (exceedingly good with hot Thai or Mexican foods; and a standard for serving up with BACK OF THE BOAT GOURMET COOKING "Strawberries dipped in Xoçai® Chocolate"), "Maywine" (my least favorite, until Christine, at the bar, suggested I try it, half and half, with club soda, and a floated strawberry; tip: eat more strawberries while drinking), and "Moscato d'Latah" (delightfully sweet and slightly effervescent). Its reds, light to full-bodied: Sangiovese, Merlot (one of the best I've tasted in the area), "Vinosity" (a unique blend of Cabernet Sauvignon, Syrah, and Zinfandel), and a "Winemaker's Reserve Red Pettit Verdot" (first in a series, and living up to its reputation as big and robust). Last but not least, there was the wonderfully sweet dessert-style red, "Natalie's Nectar."

The winery remains family-owned and operated; Mike Conway with over forty years of wine experience in management, winemaking, and vineyard know-how; Ellena devoted to accounting, fiscal, tasting room, and gift shop; their daughter, Natalie, joining in as assistant winemaker and eventually destined to take over the business.

Mike and Ellena met while in high school in southern California, Mike's aspirations of being a doctor interrupted by the Vietnam War and a four-year stint in the Air Force; Ellena and he married shortly after the end of his boot camp. Mike stationed in Ankara, Turkey, Ellena joined him there for two years.

After the military, the couple returned to California where Mike continued his schooling, at the same time taking a job as a microbiology technician for California wine behemoth E&J Gallo, followed by two years with Franzia Brothers Winery, and, then, as an assistant winemaker at Parducci. After which Ellena and he came to Washington State which was newly emerging on the wine scene, and they started Latah Creek.

The winery's grapes come from different areas in central Washington. Merlot, Cabernet, Sangiovese, and Muscat Canelli grapes grow the south-facing hills of the Wahluke Slope which boasts the longest and warmest growing seasons in the Pacific Northwest. Chardonnay grapes come from Conner Lee Vineyards, five miles south of Othello. All other grapes come from vineyards near George, overlooking the Columbia River Gorge, known for slightly cooler temperatures perfect for producing grapes of a decidedly delicate fruity nature.

Having envisioned a series of artist labels for each Latah Creek vintage, Mike and Ellena utilized the artwork of internationally acclaimed wildlife Yakima-Valley artist,

Floyd A. Broadbent, who provided them with thirteen unique labels—from wood duck to American Bald Eagle.

During our visit, the winery had its invitation-only debut of its new wine, "Monarch Red," a blend of 50% Zinfandel, 25% Cabernet, and 25% Syrah, complete with its new label, a stunningly vibrant abstract by Spokane artist Edward Gilmore. Love the artwork! As for the "Monarch Red" itself, I've still a decided preference for Latah Creek whites.

Informed that, due to the popularity of red wine in Washington State, where the winery has most of its distribution, there's presently a transitional phase ongoing to introduce more reds into the Latah Creek roster, I don't know whether to cheer or jeer, especially when I hear Mike reference his preference for "fruity" reds as opposed to "oaken." Granted, I'm in agreement with him that "oaken" can mask a lot of mistakes in winemaking, but there already just seems to be so many winemakers in Washington intent upon ferreting out simply the fruitiness for their reds that I can only hope Latah Creek's reputation for stellar whites, and its attention to them, doesn't suffer in the winery's jumping on the fruity red bandwagon. In the meantime, I'll be stockpiling all of the present Latah Creek whites in my wine cellar—just in case.

****

In our book *BACK OF THE BOAT GOURMET COOKING*, Bonnie and I paired the following Latah Creek Wine Cellars wine to go with:

Ham…Glazed with Pineapple
Latah Creek Riesling

Strawberry Spinach Salad
Latah Creek "Maywine"

Shrimp and/or Crab Cakes
Latah Creek Chardonnay

Strawberries Dipped in Xocai® Chocolate Fondue
Latah Creek Muscat Cannelli

LIBERTY LAKE CELLARS (est. 2008)

1018 S. Garry Rd.
Liberty Lake, Washington 99019
Telephone: (509) 255-9205
eMail: winemaker@libertylakewinecellars.com
Website: www.libertylakewinecellars.com

Tasting Room open on select Saturdays; call ahead.

NO ONE UNDER 21

From I-90, take Liberty Lake Exit (296).

Go south on Liberty Lake Rd., approximately one mile.

Continue straight on Garry, approximately one-half mile.

Look for winery on right.

IF YOU'RE PLANNING on tasting at more than one winery, in any one day, Liberty Lake Wine Cellars should be one put at the head of your list. Like Arbor Crest Wine Cellars, this winery has an access drive along a narrow road. Like Grande Ronde Cellars, it has a stairway to maneuver, this one steep, narrow, and wooden, complete with a turn. You won't want to be in the least inebriated when you head back on down and out.

Once you're at the end of the road, though, and at the top of those stairs, you're provided with a genuinely delightful wide-windows' grand vista, worthy, all by itself, of any and all effort you've made to get there; crushing, fermenting, storage facilities are, likewise, situated among those very same surrounding resin-fragrant pine trees directly overlooking beautiful Liberty Lake. In our case, since we were there for the winery's season Grand Opening of the summer, there was, also, a tray of substantial snacks provided on a table off to one side.

Once again, we have, here, a winery that's pretty much a sideline for its owners. Doug Smith is a Liberty Lake City employee, and his wife, Shelly, is a health-care consultant. Liberty Lake Wine Cellars arose from Doug's original efforts with home-brewed beer, sidelined when his wife, more into wine, persuaded him to experiment with twenty pounds of grapes bought at Costco. When his original wine-making efforts didn't produce wine of the same quality obtained in stores, the two began asking around, reading, and supplementing their knowledge even more by Doug taking courses at Walla Walla and Washington State University. When told so many times, by so many experts, that the real secret to any good wine, is always good grapes, usually only obtainable in bulk, the two purchased their first four tons of fruit from Walla Walla vineyards. Their 2005 vintage was released in 2008; the winery now with a maximum 500-case capacity.

The winery's specialty remains small-lot, hand-crafted, limited-edition, single-vineyard (Walla Walla and Red Mountain) red wines, all issued under a label derived from a 1926 lakeside scene vintage postcard found on eBay by the owners and personifying, in their opinion, their winery's status as part of the thriving small Liberty Lake community.

By way of our tasting, the winery offered up its debut vintage "Mountain Reds," its "Second Generation" blend (Cabernet Franc, Cabernet Sauvignon, Merlot), a Merlot, a Cabernet Sauvignon, its Cabernet Franc, and Syrah; its Syrah was sold out.

However, the same qualities—their fruitiness—that make most of these wines what they are, and have Doug and Shelly proudly boasting those as exactly what they'd hoped to conjure, as winemakers— are the same qualities that keep these wines from ever truly being anything other than just good-tasting. In fact, until Washington winemakers, and wine consumers, as a whole, stop so desperately needing, wanting, and preferring their every wine to taste predominantly of black cherries, boysenberries, raspberries, blueberries, huckleberries, strawberries, or whatever other Earth-grown berry, rather than develop more sophisticated noses and palates that explore beyond these limited fruity parameters, there won't ever be a Washington wine to compete with their more robust, complex, and long-to-age European red-vintage counterparts.

* * * * * * *

In our book *BACK OF THE BOAT GOURMET COOKING*, Bonnie and I recommended the following Liberty Lake Cellars wine to go with:

<u>Salmon on Cedar Plank</u>
Liberty Lake Cellars Syrah

LONE CANARY WINERY
(est. 2003)

NOTE: Unfortunately, by the time this book hits the stands, all of the below information for LONE CANARY WINERY will possibly be obsolete, so be sure to check before going; the winery, having been on the verge of going belly-up, and undergoing a change of ownership, is about to undergo some form of "merge" or "pairing" with Caterina Winery.

198 South Scott Street #B2
Spokane, Washington 99202
Phone# (509) 534-9062; toll free (866) 822-6279
eMail: info@lonecanary.com
Website: www.lonecanary.com

From I-90 West....

Take the Division Street exit.

Head north on Division toward downtown Spokane.

Turn right on Sprague Avenue (under the railroad tracks).

Follow Sprague Avenue for one-half mile.

Turn right on Scott Street.

Turn left into the Scott & Pacific Business Park.

Tasting Room open 12-5 P.M., Thursday-Sunday.

NO ONE UNDER 21

THE WORD IS OUT that this tasting room is closing its doors very, very soon, after a recent change of Lone Canary Winery ownership (because of acute financial difficulties), that passes it from the hands of its founder, winemaker Mike Scott, into the expanding wine empire of Don Townshend, of the very same Townshend Cellar that, also, took over Caterina Winery (without, in my opinion, any immediately favorable results). So, I made it a point to head on in to see what visitors would be missing, in the future. As it turns out, they'll be missing a very enjoyable experience, at least as far as Bonnie, Bruce, and I are concerned.

While the present Lone Canary facility is kind of out of the way, in a nondescript industrial park, its space is large and airy, and its tasting bar more than sufficiently well-manned by Patrick Kendrick who has a genuinely large working knowledge of wine, in general, and of the Lone Canary product, in particular.

I was more than interested to make Patrick's acquaintance, because, a personable young man, as well as entrepreneur (as head of Platform Booking), he used to work for Caterina Winery, before its shift into the Don Townshend expanding wine empire, and has been blamed, by way of rumor, with being in good part responsible for the Caterina repositioning within the market place, because of his introduction of beer *and* local music groups into a venue that had Caterina struggling to define itself as a winery, or as a bar, or as a place geared mainly toward showcasing local talent.

Ironic, perhaps, that Patrick informed us that he'll be moving back to Caterina, as part of the Lone Canary contingent, when the two wineries combine, supposedly to maintain separate identities, albeit under the same Don Townshend umbrella, in the renovated downtown Caterina tasting-room location.

Ironic, too, that Lone Canary's founder, Mike Scott, part of the Washington state winemaking establishment for over thirty years, helped open Caterina in 1993, and remained its general manager and winemaker until December 2002.

Mike first came to Spokane in 1980, in pursuit of a woman, but, instead, ended up working for Spokane winemaking pioneer Mike Conway, now of Latah-Creek fame, who was, then, establishing Spokane's first winery, Worden Winery, for Washington wine pioneer, Jack Worden. When Mike Conway moved on to found Latah Creek, Mike Scott went with him, later with Steve Livingstone, at Caterina, all the while honing his winemaking skills until he was approached by Steve and Jeanne Schaub for the business partnership that launched Lone Canary in 2003.

It'll be interesting to see if and how Lone Canary, without Mike's involvement and guiding hand, and how Caterina, both suddenly sharing the same ownership, production lines, and tasting space, as Townshend Cellar, retain their individuality of wines and labels.

The Lone Canary label, by the way (affectionately known as "Clooney") is a cute artistic caricature of the American Goldfinch, aka "Wild" Canary, Washington State's official bird. The idea was to come up with a winery name and logo purely indicative of the state. To be sure, they officially checked out the Washington State website and found the bird in question. Therefore, Lone Canary started out as Wild Canary until legal complications resulted from Kentucky's Wild Turkey pointing out that it owned all trademark rights to any and all "Wild" appearing, side by side, with any bird, on any alcoholic beverage. Rather than risk expensive litigation, the name change occurred. There's going to be a lot of people, myself included, sorry to see this particular bird, with its history of showcasing Sauvignon Blanc and red wines, both Italian and Bordeaux varietals, go extinct.

Being served up—by way of taster's bonanza—the day Bonnie, Bruce, and I were in attendance:

Pinot Grigio
Sauvignon Blanc
Barbera
Sangiovese
"Bird House Red" blend (Syrah, Cabernet Sauvignon, Merlot & Sangiovese)
Merlot
—and a—

Syrah—of which I purchased a bottle, because it's really quite good and lives up to what I'd been told of its uniqueness as a wine that Mike Scott had previously steered clear of, because of his penchant (also had by most of his Washington winemaker peers), to seek out only the fruitiness of every last grape, Syrah grapes having a tendency to retain an oaken quality from wine barrels. Only as a fluke, when he was offered some unsold Syrah grapes from the previous season (with its slightly cooler-than-usual "hang time"), and when he, reluctantly, went out to the vineyard to taste the grapes, did he find them surprisingly sweeter than any he remembered. The result was his limited production 148 cases of 100% Syrah, 13½% alcohol content, sweet but not overblown, with a nice acidity to keep everything in focus, and "a nose reminiscent of blackberries with faint spicy floral backdrop."

Very nice, in my opinion, and a good example of exactly what's possible when a Washington winemaker actually ventures out of his fruity-fruity-only-fruity comfort zone.

—and—

"Rouge"

"DuBrul Vineyard Reserve" blend (Merlot, Cabernet Sauvignon)

"Proprietors' Reserve" blend (Cabernet Sauvignon, Merlot, Cabernet Franc)

Late Harvest Sauvignon Blanc

—and a—

Pinot Noir (NOT FOR TASTING) of which I bought two bottles—one for Bonnie, Bruce, and I to taste (not bad!)—one for mailing to Australia to my co-author A.B.

Gayle of *WILLIAM MALTESE'S WINE TASTER'S DIARY: IN SEARCH OF THE PERFECT OZ PINOT (MORNINGTON PENINSULA)*; I suspect she's had better.

* * * * * * *

In our book *BACK OF THE BOAT GOURMET COOKING*, Bonnie and I recommended the following Lone Canary Winery wine to go with:

Catch of the Day
Lone Canary Pinot Grigio

Clams with Linguine Pasta
Lone Canary Pinot Grigio

MOUNTAIN DOME WINERY
(est. 1984)

16315 East Temple Road
Spokane, Washington 99217-9573
Telephone: 509-928-2788
eMail: gnome@mountaindome.com
Website: www.mountaindome.com

Head west on I-90 W toward Exit 281.

Take exit 281 to merge onto US-2 E/US-395 N/S Division St. toward Newport/Colville.

Continue to follow US-2 E/US-395 N.

Slight right at US-2 E/N Newport Hwy.

Turn right at WA-206 E/E Mt. Spokane Park Dr.

Turn right at N Forker Rd.

Turn left at E Temple Rd.

Destination will be on left.

Open by appointment Tuesday-Friday. Usually open Saturday, weather permitting. Call ahead.

ANY SPARKLING WINE FAN (not to be confused with a Champagne, capital "C," fan, who we all know is someone purely "into" the wines of just one particular region in France), should make Mountain Dome Winery, located on its eighty-four forested acres just outside of Spokane, in the foothills of Mt. Spokane, a decided must stop on any visit to this area's wineries. Erik Manz, sparkling winemaker, heads a winery founded by his parents, Michael and Patricia, back in 1984, and wine-makes from Pinot Noir and Chardonnay grapes in the traditional *méthode champenoise*.

Even before Bonnie, Bruce, and I, embarked upon the delightful drive into the countryside that brought us to this special winery's doorstep, I confess to having sneaked a quick taste of its most popular, non-vintage, sparkling Brut at the downtown Spokane Grande Ronde tasting room (See Grande Ronde Cellars), which, because of an incestuous business relationship that links the owners of Mountain Dome with the Grande Ronde partnership, often serves up the Mountain Dome product along with its own. Mountain Dome's sparkling wine, already highly recommended by Bonnie, at the time of my first tasting, and not a disappointment when I did taste it, saw me having left the Grande Ronde tasting room with a bottle, quickly chilled, and quickly drunk, long before I ever checked in for a sampling of the other five Mountain Dome (and fifteen Grande Ronde Cellars) wines that the Mountain Dome Mt. Spokane facility had to offer.

Mountain Dome, by the way, is called Mountain Dome not only because it sits on a "mountain," or at least on one of Mt. Spokane's many foothills, but because the family residence is nothing other than—ta-dah—a geodesic dome that adjoins the facility. Speaking of the family, the winery's non-vintage Brut sparkling wine's distinctive and fun label—a series of playful gnomes (think garden-variety) all lined up in a row, complete with pointy hats and red hair—is a tongue-in-check family portrait; although Bonnie and Bruce, having known Michael Manz, before he passed away, swear he looked exactly like the central gnome in the graphic.

The winery's first crush, a ton of Columbia River Basin grapes, including Chardonnay and Pinot, and supervised by Michael in September of 1984, was pressed in the family's kitchen and fermented in small stainless tanks. Those early experimentations continued in 1985 and 1986, with another ton of grapes, followed in 1987 by the purchase of a Willmes tank press and a crush of six tons of fruit, followed in 1988 by fermentation exclusively in small French oak barrels—accompanied by the wine-founder's philosophy: "I don't want to run a business; I want to run a winery."

If you're lucky enough to be there on a day when someone will walk you through the winery, and the sparkling-wine-making process, you'll get a rough idea of why there are so few sparkling winemakers in the state.

Firstly, few winery owners (so many in Washington with day jobs, winemaking only a hobby), have the time to devote to the decidedly special treatment such wines require; one bottle often receives as many as thirty individual turns by hand in a riddling rack, during fermentation (there's a machine at Mountain Dome that, computer-controlled, does the turning for about half the winery's production); any bottle often having had forty or fifty individual total "touches" before heading out the door.

Secondly, there's supplemental expense necessitated for equipment specifically needed for sparkling wine production, including not only the previously mentioned computer-controlled riddling rack, but temporary crown cappers for the bottles (think beer caps) while the wine is riddled to allow yeast to drain into the necks; cooling equipment to make the yeast freeze, at minus-10-degrees-Farenheit, in the necks of the bottle, before another special machine pops temporary crown caps, removes the frozen yeast, adds additional sugar, pushes a permanent cylindrical cork halfway into the neck of the bottle, mushrooms the still-extended upper half of the cork over the lip of the bottle, and then, finally, encases the newer seal with a wire muzzle to keep the cork from popping prematurely.

Thirdly, in a state of the Union wherein long-aged wine isn't in great demand, or held in any great respect, by the consumer…and, since holding wine for long periods of time is an expense few winemakers can afford…Mountain Dome manages the exceptional miracle of holding all of its non-vintage champagne two years in its bottles; vintage, four years; and—miracle of miracles—its "Cuvee Forte" for eight years. If Erik bemoans that holding his best-selling sparkling wine, his non-vintage BRUT, would likely see its quality improve tremendously, not even he is able to tie up all of the family capital that would be necessary to make that dream come true.

And for those who may wonder, as I did, why Mountain Dome's top-of-the-line sparkling wine, its "Cuvee Forte," aged for those eight years, is a non-vintage, not a vintage, it's because to each "Cuvee Forte" bottle there has been added a bit of the winery's very first 1984 production which Erik proclaims proudly, despite the family's inexperience as winemakers at the time, has become "truly wonderful; the obvious secret of great wine being great grapes from a great year."

If I came away with one complaint, it's that, as I experienced with several other area wineries, its customer services, via email and its web-site, leave a little to be desired, in that I queried them as to whether or not they would be open on one weekend, and never did receive a reply.

* * * * * * *

In our book *BACK OF THE BOAT GOURMET COOKING*, Bonnie and I recommended the following Mountain Dome Winery wine to go with:

Potatoes…with Caviar & Sour Cream
Mountain Dome "Sparkling Wine"

Pizza with Dill Cream Cheese Spread, topped with thin slices of red onion, smoked salmon, and a dollop of caviar
Mountain Dome "Sparkling Wine"

NODLAND CELLARS
(est. 2007)

11616 E. Montgomery Drive #69 & 70
Spokane Valley, Washington 99206
Phone# (509) 927-7770
eMail: ntbps@qwest.net
Website: www.nodlandcellars.com

Tasting Room open for wine festival weekends and/or by appointment.

NO ONE UNDER 21

From 1-90, take Pines Road Exit (289).

Turn North to Montgomery/Indiana.

Turn West onto Montgomery.

Drive approximately ¼ mile to the East Montgomery Commercial Center (Near the intersection of E Montgomery Dr and N Wilbur Rd.).

I ALMOST CUT THIS WINERY from this book from the get-go. As someone who majored at university in marketing/advertising, I'm a stickler for customer service. When I don't think it's being adequately provided by any company, winery or otherwise, I get genuinely turned off and figure if the company doesn't care enough to care, then why in the hell should I care about it? I've a tendency to get particularly riled when a company actually provides email software on its web-site, with the guise of being prepared to answer all questions and queries, but, it's only a ruse, in that no one is seemingly ever on the other end of the line.

Shortly after my arrival in Spokane, Nodland was scheduled to launch its new Reserve (Walla Walla Valley) Cabernet Sauvignon. Initially used for blending, the grapes had proven so special that year that some of them had been held back by Nodland specifically for Reserve bottling, released a year later. The wine's scheduled debut was by invitation-only to those on the Nodland mailing list. The only way to get on the mailing list was to buy a bottle of Nodland wine, already available, two tasting-room sessions scheduled prior to the big event. My online email question: Could I buy one of the available bottles of wine on-line, and, thereby, be placed on its mailing list...or did I have to show up in person at one of the interim two tastings? Think I could get a response? No.

Having since lodged my complaint, personally, with co-owner Tracy Nodland, who insists her husband, Jim, is the one in charge of the Nodland website...and having, afterwards, lodged my complaint, personally, with Jim...I'm still not convinced that this company's lack of customer service has been resolved. In that…Candle-artisan Jfay, who I usually commission to do one or more candles by way of accompanying the release of any of my books, emailed Nodland, just recently, to ask if there would be any objection to her displaying the Nodland Reserve Cabernet Sauvignon label, by which Jfay has been inspired, next to her candle, for public-relations purposes. Indicative of Tracy's love of art, and Jim's love of Jazz, the label's vivid graphic, done by artist Tim Rogerson, represents Tracy (glass of wine in hand) at a microphone, Jim on a guitar, a guy on saxophone, and another on piano. Think Jfay could get a response? No.

I'm still tempted to leave the winery off this list, except Tracy and Jim are genuinely likeable people, despite their lack of marketing savvy. More importantly, their products are damned good, as well as unique, as far as Washington State wines go. That I managed to realize both of the above is only because Nodland Cellars just happened to be conveniently in the vicinity of Latah Creek Wine Cellars on the very same day we were at the latter for tasting. Stopping by Nodland, on the way home, was purely spur-of-the-moment, and because of its roadside sign announcing that tastings were in progress.

Tracy, a charming hostess, was eager for us to taste the two Nodland wines available at the time. I bought a bottle of one (it proved a superb complement to an evening of our *BACK OF THE BOAT GOURMET COOKING*'s barbecued rib-eye-steak-for-three), and it put us on the Nodland mailing list for the Cabernet launch party a week away. On the spur of the moment, however, I asked if a case was available, then and there, of the Cabernet…and, as a result, loaded twelve bottles of it in the car, four bottles of which were drunk that evening, with dinner. Four to be held until next year; four to be held until the year after; since, while the wine is definitely good for drinking, now, I suspect it will be even better with just a tad more aging (unusual in most of the Washington reds).

Tracy comes from an extended Sicilian family, some of whom have been in the wine-making industry for years, but she never really had any intention of going into the business, especially upon marrying Jim Nodland, a defense lawyer. While both Tracy and Jim always enjoyed wine, it was Jim's suddenly intensified interest, triggered by one of Tracy's wine-making siblings, at an extended family reunion, that got Tracy and Jim talking about doing some on their own.

Many questions were asked by them of more experienced winemakers, including the ins and outs of the refining and fermentation processes. Classes were taken at UC Davis, Walla Walla Community College. Cabernet grapes were acquired from Walla Walla vineyards. Much experimentation and tasting ensued in their sudden search for the best wine they could make. In 2007, Nodland became the area's thirteenth (a number neither considers unlucky) winery.

Today, Nodland focuses primarily on only one wine, a red blend, each year, derived from six (sometimes seven) original Bordeaux varietal grape sources available to them in Washington State: Cabernet Sauvignon, Merlot, Cabernet Franc, Malbec, Petit Verdot, and Carménère. In these times when wine is more and more drifted into mass-production, Tracy and Jim still closely supervise every cluster of Nodland grapes to make sure it's harvested by hand, sorted by hand, cleared of debris and insects by hand (sanitation of their wine having had top priority from the get-go), crushed, barreled, blended, racked and, finally, bottled.

Pick that part of wine processing that the two can agree is most enjoyable for both of them, and it's the blending that commences after each wine has spent two years sitting in French-oak barrels. At which time, tasting begins to determine exactly what the winery has to work with. The owners share their thoughts and ideas, in that regard, as they share everything else in their lives, and set out with determination, each and every time, to marry the strengths of each wine so strengths are showcased and not overshadowed.

As a painter, as well as winemaker, Tracy has the artistic advantage of her constant and ongoing exposure to correctly mingling just the right kinds and amounts of pigments, for perfect combinations on canvas, that carries over to her putting together the right kinds and amounts of wine for the perfect Nodland pre-1870 Bordeaux old-world blends. Tracy's insistence, by the way, that she "makes wine, drinks wine, and paints wines" isn't idle boasting. She paints wine-related subject matter and, likewise, combines the purple-paste sediments from the winery's barrels with the paint mediums she uses for her canvases.

Jim's talents as a jazz musician (he paid his way through college by playing local gigs, later booking other musicians), likewise, contribute toward the thought processes that make the yearly Nodland blends pretty much unique in the Spokane area wine spectrum. Nodland's reds have far more characteristics similar to their European counterparts than do the majority of the less complex red products provided by Nodland's Spokane winery peers.

When there is an exceptionally good year for grapes, Nodland will "do" its limited production of "Bebop" dry Riesling which is usually quickly sold out. In fact, Jim pulled the very last bottle from their fridge to turn over to me for tasting. I drank it as accompaniment for the "Herb-Grilled Shrimp" from my (and Bonnie's) *BACK OF THE BOAT GOURMET COOKING*. The wine pleasantly lived up to most of its advertised "floral notes with pineapple, orange blossom, peach, pear, and green apple."

The present quick-sells of all Nodland output, Tracy and Jim not really having to go out and beat the bushes too heartily for customers, may be one reason why customer service has a tendency to exist pretty low on the company's list of priorities. If, however, production increases in the future, needing more buyers to take up the excess, the Nodlands may quickly discover their mistakes in customer service, today, may come back to bite them on the ass, sometime tomorrow.

* * * * * * *

In our book *BACK OF THE BOAT GOURMET COOKING*, Bonnie and I recommended the following Nodland Cellars wine to go with:

Herb-Grilled shrimp
Nodland Cellars "Bebop"

Oysters
Nodland Cellars "Bebop"

Rib-eye Steak
Nodland Cellars Reserve Cabernet Sauvignon

OVERBLUFF CELLARS
(est. 2009)

620 South Washington
Spokane, Washington 99204
Telephone# (509) 991-4781
eMail: john@overbluffcellars.com
Website: www.overbluffcellars.com

Call for tasting room hours, or for making an appointment.

NO ONE UNDER 21

COLOR ME IMPRESSED by this winery's customer-relations skills. There were very few other wineries as quick as this one to get back to me on my each and every query. In fact, I no sooner had a question mailed than Overbluff's owner, John Caudill, had an answer back to me; more than once, too.

    Color me equally impressed by how the Caudills have so masterfully converted the former Cobblestone Bakery, complete with charming small adjacent garden, all tucked behind an old historic Victorian-style house, into the new Overbluff tasting room.

What truly impressed me, though, was when Lynelle actually asked me, not all that long after Bonnie, Bruce, and I arrived, and had just finished tasting the winery's superior lone white-wine, its debut 100% Viognier "Vixen" made from Walla Walla Valley grapes, "Would you like to have a fresh glass for tasting our reds?" Her request was the first and last time any such offer was made by any of the Spokane wineries visited for this book. The only time I ever received a new glass, elsewhere, than at Overbluff, even a mere rinsing out of a glass between servings, at any another Spokane winery, was when I specifically asked for it to happen.

By the way, this winery's "Vixen" is only a few of the rare whites, in this whole Spokane region, I've witnessed as winning over Washington die-hard red-wine fans, like Bonnie and Bruce, plus others, like Spokane's wine-blogger "Sip of Spokane." While some attribute the wine's crossover success to its high alcohol content (16½%), we all agree that it's something decidedly more than *just* that, possibly its genuinely golden color, its "killer" legs, and just enough forward fruity flavor, backed by end-of-swallow acidity, that makes it such damned good wine, whether for hot-day summer-time drinking, or with food.

What's more, the tasting room's "Vixen" Viognier was served properly chilled, my even overhearing Lynelle comment upon how she had to check to make sure the cooling continued to be done "just right."

Let me include my appreciation for Overbluff providing more wine, per tasting, than the traditional one-ounce pour. While I see the advantage of small servings in wineries with long wine lists, no one wanting a taster to head on out drunk, Overbluff's four wines, one white and three reds, were well-served by our getting enough of each, especially the reds, to let them breathe a bit in the glass before they too quickly disappeared in swallow-downs.

Overbluff is the first area winery to use Closure System International's innovative "Alternative Wine Closures-Glass Stoppers" (glass and acrylic), not cork, not plastic, to seal its bottles. At first, I thought Lynelle introduced me to the stopper as just another way to try and preserve wine in a bottle not fully emptied the first go-round, the rest of the contents intended for later consumption. While I'm a true believer that if you're not going to drink a whole bottle at one sitting, the very best way to keep the rest, until getting back to it, is to pump out all of the existing air in the bottle neck, I was genuinely impressed by how snuggly the stopper fit, and I immediately suspected it would do better, if not more so, than most of its more elaborate counterparts. I was genuinely surprised, therefore, when informed it was "the" stopper used to seal every Overbluff bottle. Its plastic O-ring provides a tight seal, for long periods of time, and may well reduce oxygen permeation (still under testing). Its 100% inert material provides ease of opening/re-closing (no corkscrew required). Its aluminum outer cap, placed over the stopper, provides good detection of tampering. Its aesthetically pleasing look helps in Overbluff branding, and doesn't interfere (as will a screw-cap) with the de-rigueur ritual that attends most wine-bottle openings.

John Caudill's association with wine began by growing up right next door to Lodi, California's Mondavi Vineyard. It wasn't, though, until he married Lynelle, general manager of the Davenport Hotel and Tower, that his chance meeting with winemaker and wine aficionado Gerald Gibson planted the seed for formation of Overbluff Cellars. Gibson, from San Francisco, and a long-time fan of Napa Valley wines, and, though self-taught, a winemaker for over thirteen years, was buying some of Davenport Hotel's cellar to allow them to restock with newer wines. John, body manager at Camp Chevrolet, was helping Lynelle do the grunt work of delivering the Davenport bottles to Gibson, and the two men became friends. Soon, they had joined up as winemakers to produce their initial four barrels deemed good enough, by them, and by fellow drinkers, to convince them it was time to go for more.

In 2007, they produced seven barrels of Cabernet Sauvignon. In 2008, they were up to seventeen barrels, having added a Syrah and a Sémillon. Last year, it was thirty barrels, all made with a hoped-for Napa-Valley influence provided albeit via product from Walla Walla grapes.

Overbluff's official debut releases are its "Vixen" (100% Viognier); its "LaTour" (100% Cabernet Sauvignon); its "Duality" (100% Cabernet Sauvignon); and its "Reserve" (100% Cabernet Sauvignons); all three of the latter made with hopes of competing with the "big" Napa Cabernets, as opposed to the "less complex" and more fruity Washington-State Cabernets. Hurrah, guys and gal! Hurrah!

The "LaTour," in my opinion, is certainly a wine which can be enjoyed now. As for "Duality" and "Reserve," I'd prefer laying them away for at least three years to see if some of their much-appreciated tannic full-bodied qualities can be mellowed out. While Bonnie estimates that those three years would be the max, before both wines are likely to lose drinkable qualities instead of gain them, Gerald insists both wines will only be at their true peak of drinkability in about twelve years. I bought two bottles of "Duality" and "Reserve," one to drink in three years, one to drink in twelve, to see who's the better judge.

Oh, yes, Bonnie, Bruce, and I, also, picked "Vixen" as the best Spokane area Viognier any of us has tasted.

****

In our book *BACK OF THE BOAT GOURMET COOKING*, Bonnie and I recommended the following Overbluff Cellars wine to go with:

Unbelievable Shrimp Salad
Overbluff Cellars "Vixen" Viognier

Unbelievable Shrimp Salad with Penne
Overbluff Cellars "Vixen" Viognier

ROBERT KARL CELLARS (est. 1999)

115 West Pacific Avenue
Spokane, Washington 99201
Telephone: (509) 363-1353
eMail: info@robertkarl.com
Website: www.robertkarl.com

Tasting Room open 12-5 Saturday.

NO ONE UNDER 21

Take 109 to Division Street exit.

Go north three blocks to Pacific.

Turn left on Pacific.

Drive 1 block (winery located, on your left, in a 1912 fire station).

THERE IS NO ROBERT KARL. How do I know? The same way I know Robert Karl Cellars takes very seriously the concept of customer relations, somehow having managed to get back to my each and every internet query, while more than one of this area's wineries (*i.e.*, Nodland, Mountain Dome), although providing the façade of offering internet feedback, never bothered to follow through.

I let the Robert Karl Cellars know that I would likely be stopping by someday soon and was looking forward to doing so. Immediately, I got a response that the winery was looking forward to seeing me and would make it a point to open especially for me if its tasting-room hours didn't fit my schedule. I wrote back my thanks to "Mr. Karl" for his goodness-graciousness, but said I always try not to put any winery to extra bother and would, likely, just drop by with the rest of the public.

The immediate come-back was that it wasn't Mr. Karl on the other end of the internet connect, but Rebecca Gunselman; no Robert, either—only Joe, Rebecca's husband. "Robert" merely taken from her side of the family, "Karl" from her husband's side of the family, when the Gunselmans' marketing research decided the most-bought wines were those that people didn't have any difficulty in pronouncing: a philosophy that, if it came into question over the years, especially with so many queries as to why they didn't name the winery after themselves, proved valid the year they produced a special wine release, named "Gunselman," and had customers merely pointing and saying, "I'll have a bottle of...er...that wine...er...that begins with 'G'."

Rebecca, in attendance on the Saturday we checked in, proved just as affable in person as she did over the internet, quickly providing us with a brief history of the winery while lining up our glasses for the five wines on that day's tasting list—Claret, Merlot, Syrah, Cabernet Sauvignon, and "Inspiration" blend.

If the tasting area consists primarily of an upturned wine barrel, topped by a piece of plate glass, the rest of the space occupied by the winery's production facility, this will change when production is moved to the available acre at the Gunselman Bench Vineyard, and the Spokane building is converted into just a tasting room and event facility. Speaking of the building, it's a marvelous structure, once used by an early (1912) Spokane fire department with horse-drawn wagon. The winery logo includes two horse heads to tie Robert Karl not only to its Horse-Heaven Hills connection but to the fire-station horses once housed on-site.

Rebecca's walk-through of the premises—a virtual Winemaking 101 course, including viewing of sorting bin, de-stemmer, fermentation tanks, press, barrels, and bottling—is worth the trip, in itself, especially for any home-winemaker with aspirations for going public.

Rebecca's graciousness toward her fellow region winemakers was noted and appreciated, in that she always had something favorable to say about each and every one of them that came up in conversation, recommending her competitor's Whitestone downtown tasting room, and even attempting to rationalize the possible reasons behind the horrid experience we had at the "Grand Opening" of Caterina by suggesting we give new owner Don Townshend a bit more time to "make those wines his own."

The Gunselmans, long-time wine fans, although Joe's "official" career is as an anesthesiologist, moved to Spokane in 1998, looking to set up a winery as a sideline, after having helped friends plant a vineyard in Virginia, believing Washington State provided the country's very best grapes, and deciding Spokane provided the ideal environment for raising their three boys.

Their first wines resulted from grapes brought in from Central Washington vineyards, as well as from the Whitestone vineyards, on Lake Roosevelt, before the latter started reserving its total output exclusively for making Whitestone wines.

Eventually, Joe and Rebecca were convinced the Horse Heavens Hills area of south-central Washington provides the perfect growing conditions for Cabernet Franc, Cabernet Sauvignon, Petite Verdot, Merlot, Malbec, Syrah, and Savignon Blanc grapes. Besides which, they were continually drawn back to that specific area by the way the soil clumped up around their boots, and by the way the wind whipped through the landscape. As a result, they purchased eight acres of land, there, and planted seven acres of it with Cabernet Sauvignon grapes to found Gunselman Bench Vineyard. Likewise, two of the other area vineyards, McKinley Springs, and Phinny Hill, agreed to plant and long-lease blocks of grapes exclusively for use by Rebecca and Joe. By 2003, Robert Karl's total production was from grapes one hundred percent from those three Horse Heaven Hills vineyards, and from Andrews Horse Heaven Ranch, with the winery's flagship wine being its Cabernet Sauvignon, its "workhorse" wine being its popular Claret.

Although Rebecca was quick to point out that the winery's oak barrels were, typical of Washington winemakers, meant to provide "only the slightest hint of oak flavor," I was surprised and pleased to find the twenty-four-month aged Cabernet Sauvignon replete with more-than-usual sophisticated hints of tannin, briar, earth, mocha/chocolate, and, yes, cherry. A bottle of the "Inspiration" five-grape Bordeaux blend, dark, dense, and redolent with nuances of raspberry, Bing cherries, even hints of cassis and black olives, proved "the" wine by way of perfect accompaniment for Bonnie and my *BACK OF THE BOAT GOURMET COOKING* recipe for grilled salmon. The Robert Karl Claret, also, a blend of five wines, with hints of mocha/chocolate, evergreen/eucalyptus, even a trace of mint, was another pleasant surprise that I can well imagine drinkers enjoying even without needing any kind of food in accompaniment.

A special treat for me, however, as a result of my ongoing complaint that there seems a dearth of white wines within this region's output, was Rebecca's revelation that Robert Karl occasionally does, if faced with a good grape year, produce a white, one of which, its Sauvignon Blanc, was on the brink of official release. What's more, she graciously retrieved a bottle of it from the back room for me to take away, by way of sneak preview.

I've always been a fan of Sauvignon, although its many possible flavors (from mown grass, bell peppers, vanilla, even to passion fruit), often confuses a lot of consumers, and results in it having less of a following than the more taste-consistent whites, like Chardonnay. However, I'm surprised that it's not more popular with Washington drinkers if just because it's a wine that can be drunk so young, without extensive aging (although I have found it aged for as long as fifteen years, the resulting creamy lusciousness truly stunning). Its usually high acidity keeps its possible sweetness from ever being too cloying or sticky. It pairs so well with so many strong foods that can overpower other whites that I find it a particular favorite of mine for accompanying salmon. In fact, the Karl Roberts Sauvignon Blanc, with its clean, bright, fresh, lively and crisp lean toward a fresh fruit nose and palate (melons, mangos, oranges, kiwis, apples—which I've come to expect of most Washington wines), rather than herbal flavors, went very well by way of pairing with Bonnie and my *BACK OF THE BOAT COOKING* grilled salmon.

****

In our book *BACK OF THE BOAT GOURMET COOKING*, Bonnie and I recommended the following Robert Karl Cellars wine to go with:

Grilled Salmon
Robert Karl Cellars "Inspiration"
(+ try it with Robert Karl Cellars Sauvignon Blanc)

Herb Pasta
Robert Karl Cellars Sauvignon Blanc

VINTAGE HILL CELLARS (est. 2006)

319 W. 2nd
Spokane Washington 99201
Located near downtown, 3½ blocks west of Division on 2nd, on the south side of this one-way, westbound street.
Telephone: (509) 624-3792
eMail: (See Website)
Website: www.vintagehillcellars.com

Tasting Room (who the hell knows?)

NO ONE UNDER 21

THIS WINERY is one I put in the very same boat as Emvy Cellars, Masset Winery, and Morrison Lane, all three of the latter associated with the Grande Ronde tasting-room collective; all four, in my opinion, warranting only brief mention.

I just don't feel Vintage Hills Cellars presently provides enough "presence" and/or "availability" within the Spokane/Pullman WA wine area to recommend it in a wine-tasting guide, like this one. In fact, the result of a collaboration and friendship between a commercial realtor and a political advisor, both come at wine-making primarily as a hobby, rather than a full-time-profession, its tasting room wasn't open on any of the three separate weekends we stopped by. What's worse, I heard reports from some who have found it open that they never plan to return, "ever again," not necessarily because of an inferior product but because of the less-than-customer-friendly attitude of whomever was behind the service counter.

While I have it on the authority of local blogger "DrinkNectar" (aka Josh Wade) that some of this winery's wine comes with exceptional "nose" more complex and full-bodied than from many of the larger production facilities located in central Washington, you couldn't prove it by me, or by anyone else, aside from Josh who was the only person I could ever track down who had ever sampled the product.

WHITESTONE WINERY
(est. 1992)

111 S. Cedar (between 1st (one-way going east), and 2nd (one-way going west)
Spokane, Washington 99201
Telephone: (509) 838-2427
eMail: msh@whitestonewinery.com
Website: www.whitestonewinery.com

Tasting Room (call for hours)

NO ONE UNDER 21

THERE ARE A LOT OF THINGS I genuinely like about Whitestone Winery. I like its history (fascinating), its downtown tasting room (charming, intimate bistro ambience with wine-barrel tables, lounge area, bar, and often live jazz), its winemaker (gregarious, friendly, chockablock with interesting information), its winemaker's wife (a pharmacology major who sees the irony of the existent drug/alcohol dichotomy), and, last but not least, its decidedly fine red wines (made entirely of grapes from its own vineyard). The only thing that would make me like this winery better is if its winemaker didn't have such a distain for white wines, because, considering what he's managed to do with Whitestone Washington reds, I think he could provide some genuinely outstanding Washington whites if he ever put his mind to it.

The Whitestone vineyard is located within the shadow of Whitestone Rock on the shores of eastern Washington's Lake Roosevelt. The lake stretches about 150 miles from Grand Coulee Dam (upstream) to the Canadian border, making it one of the state's largest lakes with over 630 miles of shoreline. For a long while, the area was known primarily for its excellent water sports, wildlife, fishing, bird-watching, photography, even star-gazing. What it has since become known for—and to everyone's surprise, was *once before known for,* but had become long-time forgotten—is its capacity to provide high-quality grapes.

In 1992, Walter and Judy Haig were entertaining friends on the deck of their Lake Roosevelt summer home, when the conversation turned to the history of the land thereabouts. The Haigs pulled out a scrapbook of the area, handed down from the original homesteader of their property, in which an old U.S. agricultural map identified the crops planted there at the turn of the eighteenth century. To everyone's surprise, wine grapes, nowhere to be seen in 1992, were highlighted. Curious as to the apparent anomaly, the Haigs, wine enthusiasts since the early 1970s when they'd been living in Santa Barbara, California, contacted Washington State University's expert viticulturist Robert Wample for a hoped-for explanation.

As it turned out, the area currently around the Whitestone vineyard had once been one of "the" most prolific grape-growing and orchard regions in the state before the construction of the Grand Coulee Dam had inundated vineyard and orchard alike and, somehow, erased most memory of them in the process.

A brief resurrection of the facts, surrounding the area's grape-growing potential, did occur in 1970 when Walter Clore (since recognized as the "Father of Washington Wine"), performed a study on the lower Lake Roosevelt area, from the confluence of the Spokane and Columbia rivers, and recognized its potential as a major viniculture region. Few paid attention, though, until the Haigs ferreted out his information that pinpointed how their property, now aided by its adjacency to Lake Roosevelt, had just the microclimate environment…four distinct seasons, highlighted by long and sunny summer days, cool nights, and temperature differentials from mid-September to early November with ten to fifteen degrees warmer than areas farther from the water…perfect for well-balanced and mature Bordeaux varietal grapes.

Not people to do things half-assed, the Haigs spent the next two years doing research, and pre-planning, before even one single vine…of the 21,000 initially planted, via hand-augured holes thirty-inches deep to maximize water and provide freeze protection…was put to ground. Attention was given to providing not only the perfect nine-foot row spacing, but to orientation of all those rows in order to provide for the best airflows and sunlight.

While initially all of the Haigs resulting grape harvests were sold to wineries in the Walla Walla, Washington, area, eventually the Haigs purchased and renovated an old service station, in the nearby town of Wilbur, Washington, which they used to produce a small batch of Whitestone

Winery Merlot. Not only did they have the advantage of their grapes being home-grown, but, of having their chief winemaker, their son, Michael, home-grown as well. Having been there from the get-go to help his parents plant the vineyard, harvest the crops, and deliver the grapes to the wineries in Walla Walla, Michael learned first-hand about winemaking from some of the area's best vintners, while, also, getting Accounting and Economics degrees; all of which had him ideally positioned when the Haigs decided to start Whitestone and "run" with it.

After 2004, and since, all Haig grapes have become channeled exclusively into Whitestone Winery products. Whitestone doesn't supplement with any fruit from any other source, either, and are one hundred percent estate-bottled. They pick their fruit only when it's ready and small-batch ferment using different yeast strains and barrels to create unique components for their blending.

They opened their downtown Spokane tasting room in April 2009. The afternoon we were there, Michael provided tasting of two Whitestone blends, "Pieces of Red" (fruity with peppery undertones) and "Lake Roosevelt Red" (surprisingly tannic—hurrah!—for a Washington wine, and begging for a large piece of rare steak to go with it), as well as their Cabernet Sauvignon (tannins with hints of chocolate and coffee), Merlot (more fruit, more pepper), and Cabernet Franc (refreshingly tart, with hints of berry). He was assisted by his wife Sarah, while his parents made the rounds of the room, a jazz combo played convivial music at the front of the house, and a woman took the microphone to sing "Over the Rainbow." That I didn't mind the latter, "Rainbow" NOT one of my favorite songs, was as good an indication of any that I was enjoying myself and the bottle of Cabernet Sauvignon we'd ordered served up at our table.

We left with a bottle of the Cabernet Franc which Bonnie and I believed at the time, and later confirmed, would provide wondrous accompaniment to the grilled-pizza recipe in our *BACK OF THE BOAT GOURMET COOKING*.

* * * * * * *

In our book *BACK OF THE BOAT GOURMET COOKING*, Bonnie and I recommended the following Whitestone Winery wine to go with:

Beef Steak...Rib-eye
Whitestone Winery Cabernet Sauvignon
(+ try it with Whitestone Winery "Lake Roosevelt Red"

Inside-Out Bleu-Cheese Buffalo Burger
Whitestone Winery "Lake Roosevelt Red"

Nachos
Whitestone Winery Merlot

Pizza
Whitestone Cabernet Franc

Ribs...Country
Whitestone Winery Cabernet Franc

Salmon...Cedar Plank
Whitestone "Pieces of Red v. 6.022-"

COLBERT AND MEAD (GREENBLUFF), WASHINGTON

COLBERT AND MEAD (GREENBLUFF), Washington, is a rural area, in the rolling Spokane Mountain foothills, northeast of Spokane, composed of an association of small family farms and food stands, which originally formed in 1902 as a way of protecting local strawberry growers from outside competition, but has since evolved into promoting agricultural tourism with the promise of "an old-fashion farm experience."

What makes Greenbluff so unique in the whole United States is its large concentration of over thirty farms within a relatively small twelve-square-mile area.

If you're from the city and never had an opportunity to pick your own fruit, Greenbluff provides just that opportunity, via two loops, the West and the East, each full of small farms catering to any city-slicker's penchant for seeking out "the bucolic rural experience." Arrive in early August, and you can buy apricots picked less than an hour before you arrive. October is the annual Apple Festival which started a couple of decades ago as a one-day celebration since metamorphosed into six-weeks of all-out apple (Jonagolds, Granny Smith, Fuji) frenzy, complete with live music, hayrides, corn mazes, pony rides and petting zoos. Sandwiched in between, there's the July Cherry Festival, Cherry Pickers' Trot and Pit Spit, and the August Peach Festival.

The area's unique geographical traits allow extensive dry-farming (non-use of irrigation), that provides exceptionally delicious and plentiful product.

If I've not yet mentioned grapes, read on, until you come to Trezzi Wine.

COLBERT AND MEAD (GREEN-BLUFF), WASHINGTON WINERIES

TERRANOVA CELLARS
(est. 2009)

18102 North Day Mount Spokane Road
Mead, Washington 99021
Telephone: (509) 720-7002
eMail: terranovacellars@gmail.com
Website: www.terranovacellars.com

Take exit 281.

Merge onto US-2 E/US-395 N/S Division St toward Newport/Colville N.

Continue to follow US-2 E/US-395 N.

Slight right at US-2 E/N Newport Hwy.

Turn right at E Day Mt Spokane Rd.

Destination will be on the right.

Tasting Room Hours: Most weekends. (Seasonal) 12-6 Friday, Saturday, and Sunday, or make an appointment.

I WAITED AN EXTRA week before finishing this *WINE TASTER'S DIARY* edition, and sending it off to my publishers, just so I could, hopefully, include this winery which, in the process of transferring its facilities to northern Spokane's Greenbluff area, from central Washington's Walla Walla, ran into red-tape entanglements that kept it from opening as early this year as originally planned.

Animal-lover that I am, I just can't help finding something extremely appealing about a winery named in tribute to Brent and Heidi Bendick's Newfoundland dogs which they consider benevolent, gentle, playful, strong, loyal—in effect, the epitome of all things the young winemakers hope to instill in Terranova Cellars' wines. See the doggie on the Terranova Cellars wine labels!? A portion of all wine sales are donated to a fund set up to rescue Newfoundlands; so, you can not only enjoy a good drinking experience but know that you're saving a canine's life at one and the same time. Good feelings all around. Positive vibes! Nice!

Brent came to Spokane, via Walla Walla, where he worked as an assistant winemaker for Isenhower Cellars, via Colorado, where he worked and consulted in Information Technology after his graduation from the University of Puget Sound. He and Heidi were looking for a way to combine their love of wine and winemaking with other things that were genuinely of importance to them, like family (two children, another on the way), hard work, good fun, and a hoped-for chance to help rescue Newfoundlands (the couple have two, Lalique and Recco—oh, yes, a Saint Bernard, Sadie, as well). The Spokane area, with its quickly developing and thriving wine community, along with its mountains, lakes, and scenic parks, all in close proximity, seemed ideally suited for the kind of healthy family-oriented environment for which the Bendicks were looking.

Heidi, officially the "assistant winemaker and tasting-room manager," has an MBA from Spokane's Gonzaga University, as well as a 10-year career in the insurance industry.

The couple handpicks all of the winery grapes from the Elerding, Horse Heaven Hills, Kiona, Red Mountain, and Sagemoor vineyards in the eastern Washington's Columbia Valley region, transports them to their Greenbluff facility in one-half ton bins, ferments in open top containers, and ages in 225-liter French and American oak barrels for twelve-to-twenty months before bottling.

We tasted its Barbera, Cabernet, "Rosé," "Red Table Wine," Sangiovese, and 100% Tempranillo. Bruce prefers its Barbera to that from the locally grown grapes at Trezzi Farm, just down the road, but, the latter remains my particular favorite. Both of us agreed that the Terranova "Red Table Wine" deserved more experimentation, maybe with a pizza or hamburger (which proved very nice, indeed!), so took away a bottle of that, as well as a bottle of the Sangiovese; the latter, as expected, was an excellent pairing for the "Bruschetta with Classic Tomato Basal Topping" from Bonnie and my *BACK OF THE BOAT GOURMET COOKING* (although too late to actually make that recommendation in that book).

TOWNSHEND CELLAR
(est. 1998)

16112 North Greenbluff Road
Colbert, Washington 99005
Telephone: (509) 238 1400
eMail: info@townshendcellar.com
Website: www.townshendcellar.com

From I-90 take 281 exit.

Merge onto US-2 E/US-395 N/S Division St.

Continue to follow US-2 E/US-395 N.

Slight right at US-2 E/N Newport Highway.

Turn right on E Day Mt. Spokane RD/E Greenbluff Rd.

Turn left at E Day Mt. Spokane Rd.

Turn left at N Halliday Rd.

Turn left to stay on N Halliday Rd.

Take the 1st right onto Greenbluff Dr.

EVERYONE'S OPINION OF any wine is subjective, as, apparently, is everyone's opinion of Don Townshend of Townshend Cellar. I may like a wine that you need to dump after your first taste, and vice-versa. To some...like Davide and Stephanie Trezzi who have seen Don make their Trezzi wines a reality...like Lone Canary Winery and Caterina Winery, both having faced bankruptcy, only to be rescued from oblivion by Don...like Jill Rider, general manager of Townshend Cellar...like I, who found him prompt, courteous, and informative, as regards a query I made to him, regarding the possibility of ice wine from the Barbera grapes locally grown in Greenbluff, Washington...the man is a mentor, a knight in shining armor, a superb boss, and someone who, unlike some of his competitors, obviously knows the value of good customer relations. To others, though, he's merely a megalomaniac, corporate raider, white shark, leviathan, behemoth, of the Spokane/Pullman wine district, out to gobble up the competition and make his already decidedly large wine empire (20,000 cases a year, twenty-five different wines) all the more extensive.

In 1979, Townshend worked with Preston Winery, in the Tri-Cities, Washington, area, but, surprisingly enough, not as a winemaker but as part of the team installing an air-chiller unit. When he moved to Greenbluff, Washington, ten years later, exposed to the local orchards of apples, apricots, peaches, and pears, alongside strawberries and raspberries, his original intention was to make wines from those, but he soon discovered the complexities and costs of doing so were just too prohibitive. As a result, he decided, in 1995, to test his hand at making more traditional wines and proceeded to do so with his first barrel of Cabernet and another of Merlot, bottled in 1998, released in 2001 along with a 2001 Chardonnay, and a "Huckleberry Port"; the latter made from locally grown berries. The Cabernet won the *Wine Press Northwest*'s Fab Cab Award in 2003 in a competition that included product from far older and far longer established wineries. Townshend Cellar is the giant it is today because of Townshend's continued wine-making abilities combined with his obviously extraordinary shrewd business and marketing sense.

What surprised me, and surprises most people, upon arrival at the decidedly pleasant and welcoming (charming and knowledgeable Jill Rider behind the serving bar) Townshend Cellar tasting room, adjacent to the winery, in the Mt. Spokane foothills (a wondrous rolling landscape spilling into the horizon outside the large picture windows), is the truly enormous scope of the Townshend wines being offered, from a…be still my beating breast… FREE tasting list (fourteen wines, ranging from Sauvignon Blanc, Viognier, Syrah, Merlot, "Huckleberry Blush," to "T3," the latter a non-vintage Bordeaux blend of Cabernet Sauvignon, Merlot, and Cabernet Franc initially sold only to restaurants), to a $5 fee menu that offered any four choices from thirteen additional wines (actually, only twelve, in that the Cabernet Franc was sold out), like the "Huckleberry Brut Sparkling Wine," Pinot Noir, Lemberger, Tempranillo, Malbec, Late Harvest Viognier, Late Harvest Gewürztraminer, and "Huckleberry Port."

The advantages to the vast selection, of course, is that even the pickiest drinker is likely to find at least one wine that's so good that he or she has to take a bottle home; none of the bottles priced over thirty dollars, by the way. Townshend learned early on that since he wasn't going to be able to charge big prices for small output, his best alternative was large output at cheaper prices. None of which means, this winemaker necessarily skimps in his attempt to provide quality for the bucks paid out to drink it. Some of Townshend wines spend thirty months in oak barrels, another three to four years in bottles, before they're released. Truly rare for any Spokane/Pullman area winery. At the time I was there, he was just turning out a Cabernet after holding it back for seven years, seeming to provide credence to his often voiced philosophy that he's "committed to quality wine released when it's ready, not when the cost sheet says so."

Also, at the time I was there, ground-breaking was occurring on a new and larger tasting room, located farther north. Although the existing location was voted by *Tasting Room Magazine* as one of the top ten places in the area to picnic, the expansion will allow twenty acres, with some spectacular views, to be made available for weddings, parties, and business meetings.

Winery and tasting room eventually to become the legacy of Don's two sons, Michael and Brendon, both deeply involved in the business, and whom Don hopes will one day take over the helm—when and if he's willing to release it.

****

In our book *BACK OF THE BOAT GOURMET COOKING*, Bonnie and I recommended the following Townshend Cellar wines to go with:

Chicken, Fiesta Tequila Lime
Townshend Cellar Sauvignon Blanc
Townshend Cellar Chardonnay

Decadent Chocolate Dessert Pizza
Townshend Cellar "Huckleberry Port"

Inside-Out Bleu-Cheese Buffalo Burger
Townshend Cellar Malbec

Inside-Out Burger
Townshend Cellar Cabernet Sauvignon

Rib-eye Steak
Townshend Cellar "Reserve"

Ribs…Country
Townshend Cellar Lemberger

TREZZI WINE
(est. 2009)

7700 North Dunn Road
Colbert, Washington 99005
Phone# (509) 238 2276 / (509) 979-7576
eMail: divide_stephanie@yahoo.com
Website: www.trezzifarm.com

From I-90 take 281 exit.

Merge with US-2 E/US-395 N/S Division Street toward Newport/Colville N.

Continue to follow US-2 E/US 395 N.

Slight right at US-2 E/Newport Highway.

Turn right at E Day Mt. Spokane Rd.

Turn left at N Greenbluff Rd.

Slight right to stay on North Greenbluff Rd.

Turn right at N Dunn Rd.

"GET THEE TO TREZZI WINERY!" if you're anywhere near, and if you do, you won't be sorry, if just because this is the only local winery I found (with the exception of Arbor Crest with its small vineyard of "sparkling wine" grapes on its Spokane Valley hillside location), that actually makes its wines from grapes grown on-site. Most of the area's wineries haul their grapes in from Central Washington. Even Whitestone Winery, which can, and does, as it very well should, boast wine production one-hundred percent from its very own vineyard, has its grapes growing more than sixty-six miles away.

There is just something genuinely appealing to someone like I, admittedly at times too jaded for my own good, stumbling, however accidentally, upon someplace like Trezzi Wine, which wasn't officially listed in any of the State advertising literature, only in "A Guide to Special Events and Farm Fresh Produce at Greenbluff." In fact, its wine was seemingly only tacked on—TREZZI FARM FOOD & WINE—as kind of an afterthought. If it hadn't been for Bonnie and Bruce, who frequent the Greenbluff area, at all times of the year, for fresh produce, and who knew Trezzi had its wine going for it besides its superb homemade Italian take-home frozen foods (the latter having Bonnie and me considering Davide and Stephanie true experts in authentic rustic Italian cuisine), I would have missed out on a genuinely enjoyable experience…prefaced by my frequent, "Are you sure there's actually a winery making wine from local grapes, anywhere around here?"

Suddenly, though, by the side of the road, there appeared not fruit trees but the first of the grape vines visible on the twenty-two acres of Trezzi farmland. At the end of the lead-in dirt road, there appeared, above a slight rise in the ground, the two red-roofed barns—one, large; one, small—as well as the very large metal-sculpture rooster in the parking area (I noted a second similar fowl off to one side), all immediately providing me marvelous recall of the many wonderful experiences I've had wining and dining throughout northern Italy that looks so very much just like this does. Okay, in these days when outward showings of American patriotism are often looked upon as excessive, I admit to being equally moved by the flagpole flying the Stars and Stripes.

The larger red-roofed barn, entered first, had nothing to do with wine. What predominated, first step inside its door, were those marvelous smells I've come to associate with Italian kitchens. Likewise enjoying the mouth-watering aromas was the line-up of people there to pick up any and all of the available home-cooked, packaged, and frozen Italian foods, ranging from meatballs to minestrone soup. It was while I was detoured into purchasing a two-lb package of Trezzi Farm homemade Meat Lasagna, Bruce and Bonnie doing the very same, that Davide unassumingly asked if we'd be interested in wine-tasting. There's no doubt in my mind that he seemed genuinely surprised, and showed it, when I confessed that his wine, not his food, was my chief reason for being there.

At which point, we exited to the outside and over to the smaller tractor barn, converted into tasting room and entertaining facility. While we were the only people there, I can't imagine that the case once word gets out, although Davide and Stephanie seemed genuinely disconcerted that wide-word might, indeed, get out, and risk their losing their much-cherished small family-farm "feel" to some kind of disruption caused by increased demand for their products (wine, food, or otherwise). Presently, they're a one-man, one-woman, operation, and they'd really like to keep it that way if they possibly can.

Davide is originally from Milan. Stephanie is a California girl. They met in Italy when she was on holiday. If it was love at first sight, he still showed up in America three weeks after her return home so that they could make sure their love was long-lasting and not something short-lived and merely spawned by romantic Italy, a handsome and charming Italian man, a pretty American gal, and the interaction of the two over a few short days of vacation. Deciding they were truly in love, it was then a case of where to live—the U.S., or Italy. Since Davide had always had dreams of living in the U.S., the two ended up here, eventually in Greenbluff because of its rural and rustic charm.

If their initial business success came from their food and catering skills, the Greenbluff area reputed to be way too cold for grape-growing...hey, Davide is an Italian, isn't he, and it wasn't long before he'd persuaded Stephanie that they should hand-plant (they used labor-intensive post-hole tools, instead of augers), a small vineyard of Northern Italian reds. With some good advice offered by John Simpson of Madeira, California, the vineyard actually flourished. With some additional friendly input from nearby Don Townshend of Townshend Cellar (which has its production facilities three miles away, in Greenbluff, although its grapes are all rounded up from Washington's central Columbia valley), the first limited release of ruby-hued, bold-and-spicy, Trezzi Farm Estate Barbera was realized.

For all that I've said in this book, regarding Don Townshend and/or Townshend Cellar (I thought he handled his Grand Opening of Caterina horribly, if you remember, and I'm still awaiting the outcome of his recent takeover of Lone Canary), there's no denying his long-held part, mainly favorable, within the Spokane/Pullman Wine Region's wine-producing on-going saga. What's more, his mentoring of wineries like Trezzi is certainly commendable, not only in his having helped it bottle and launch its on-site estate Trezzi Barbera but in, likewise, having given them the assist to launch their Columbia Valley "White Rooster" (remember the metal sculptures in the Trezzi surrounds?) Sauvignon Blanc.

While Bonnie, Bruce, and I didn't find anything exceptional about the Trezzi Sauvignon Blanc, made from imported Columbia Valley grapes, while we're heavy with our kudos and encouragement for the locally grown Trezzi Barbera, there's no denying the benefit to the winery (and catering service) of having at least one Trezzi white wine on its menu before the Trezzi winery's Pinot Grigio vines, just planted, hopefully survive the area's brutal winters and produce their grapes for another exceptionally locally grown Greenbluff wine—this time a white one.

By way of those mentioned cold winters, Trezzi had for the two years previous to my stop-by lost some two-thirds of its Barbera grape crops to early freezes. Curious as to the potential of using any such future frozen grapes to make "ice" wine, although assured by the Trezzis that the Barbera grape isn't geared for any such production, even though I was aware that some red grapes (Merlot, for instance) are, albeit rarely, used, I put the question to Don Townshend, himself, who I figured knew the area and the grapes, including the Trezzi grapes, well enough to give me the specifics I was after. Sure enough:

"The trick with ice wine," Don told me, "is to have both reasonable sugar levels and reasonable acidity. If the grapes get clobbered early due to frost, the sugar levels typically are not high enough and the acid levels are also extremely high. The process of late harvest and ice wine is in the dehydration of the grapes which removes water but leaves the sugars and the acids. This creates the high sugar content in the grapes. If sugars are low to start with, it's not feasible to produce what you are looking for, along with the fact that the flavors of the grape are not mature and they are also very tart. Not to say it can't be done but most likely it would not turn out the best."

****

In our book *BACK OF THE BOAT GOURMET COOKING*, Bonnie and I recommended the following Trezzi wine to go with:

Penne with Tomato Mozzarella and Basil
Trezzi "White Rooster Sauvignon Blanc"

Pizza, Traditional
Trezzi Farm "Estate Barbera"

THE PALOUSE AREA, WASHINGTON

DON'T DARE VISIT eastern Washington and merely end it in Spokane without heading out on the day trip that'll take you to the three wineries in this Palouse-area corner of the state. It's here, if you're a true wine aficionado, and a fan of the same "kind" of wines you'll find throughout France, with complexities and sophisticated "noses," that you'll find just what you're looking for. Especially highlight Merry Cellars and Wawawai Canyon Winery on your agenda, both located in Pullman, as must-stop destinations on any genuine wine lover's tour.

Certainly, don't be distracted by anyone who tells you the Palouse area of southeastern Washington is exceptional only because of its extensive fields of wheat and lentils, or for the rivalry existing, there, between two close-proximity universities—Washington State University (my alma mater), Pullman, and the University of Idaho (Moscow). In fact, it's just its unique combination of local agrarian and academic expertise that may make this newest of the Washington State wine districts one of "the" primary wine destinations in the whole Pacific Northwest.

About thirty miles to the south of Pullman, 1,600 feet downhill, is the Lewiston-Clarkston Valley, whose temperatures average seven degrees higher than the surrounding area; that fact made it, a century ago, a thriving grape-growing and wine-producing region later ruined by the onset of Prohibition that replaced vineyards with orchards. Now, though, there's a resurgence of interest in reintroducing vineyards that has some of the current local grape crops used in the exceptional blends produced by the wineries of the area. Whether it's that, or the use of Hungarian oak barrels (many queried Spokane winemakers, with the exception of Barili Cellars, seemed unfamiliar with their existence), that provides for the uniqueness of Wawawai Canyon Winery's and Merry Cellar Winery's blends...or, in the final analysis, if it's merely cases of winemakers being at the top of their craft...there is definitely something about many of this area's wines, the majority of its grape content, like elsewhere in eastern Washington, imported from the more profuse-growing vineyards of central Washington, that make it special.

NOTE: If you can, take a picnic lunch and arrange to be at Wawawai Canyon Winery when it opens at eleven.

Head on from there to Clarkston's Basalt Cellars.

Make sure, though, that you budget your time wisely, in order to make it back to Pullman before Merry Cellars closes.

While we thought five hours was more than enough time to see three wineries, and that small towns would be easy to maneuver, we were mistaken on both counts.

PULLMAN, WASHINGTON

PULLMAN IS A COLLEGE TOWN (Washington State University, my alma mater), located some seventy-six miles southeast of Spokane in the state's Palouse agricultural region first inhabited by Native Americans, visited by Lewis and Clark, who passed through on their journey to the mouth of the Columbia, and with at least two different accounts of how the city, originally Three Forks, was founded. Either, in 1875, Bolin Farr positioned his ranch at the confluence of the Missouri Flat Creek, Dry Fork, and South Fork of the Palouse River...or, in 1877, Daniel G. McKenzie of Kansas set down roots. Either way, a community arose around whichever the first homestead, in part because of the artesian wells found in the area. A post office was established in 1881, and a name-change to Pullman occurred, in honor of George Pullman, railroad sleeping car tycoon, for apparently no other reason than that the founding fathers were casting around for someone of the day appropriately famous after whom to name their town.

    It incorporated in 1886, with a population of 250 people. In 1890, it received its land-grant for Washington State College (its rural credentials having it long affectionately known as Pullman "*Cow*-lege"), with only a few dozen students, which eventually evolved into university status (initially affectionately known as "WS-*Mooooooooooo*"), with its thousands of co-eds in attendance today.

Pullman is, also, known as "the" home of the National Lentil Festival. Notice, that's not the home of the "National Grape Festival." The city's two wineries, like the majority of this district's other wineries, with the rare exceptions mentioned, import their grapes for crushing from the more prolific vineyards of central Washington.

PULLMAN, WASHINGTON WINERIES

MERRY CELLARS
(est. 2004)

1300 N.E. Henley Court
Pullman, WA 99163
Mailing Address: PO Box 776 Pullman WA 99163
Telephone: (509) 338-4699
eMail: bemerry@merrycellars.com
Website: www.merrycellars.com/contact.php

Take exit #279.

Merge onto US-195 S toward Colfax/Pullman.

Turn left at WA-270 E.

Turn right at WA-270E/Davis Way.

Turn right at N Grand Ave.

Turn left at SE Paradise St (signs for State Route 270E/WSU/Moscow).

Destination on right.

Tasting Room Hours: 1-6 Tuesday through Saturday and by appointment.

WE ARRIVED LATE...I mean *really* late...I mean around seven o'clock in the evening, late; an hour after official closing. Not the way we planned it. In fact, Merry Cellars was originally the very first winery on our intended list of to-visits in the Pullman/Clarkston, Palouse area. Since, however, we had initially arrived in Pullman earlier than the tasting room's official opening (one P.M.), we had detoured to Wawawai Canyon Winery to taste there, and enjoy our picnic lunch in its superb recreational room, with an accompanying bottle of its wine. Tasting and lunch finished, we'd again headed off to Merry Cellars, frustrated by our Global Positioning System whose pleasant female voice kept insisting that we were "out of bounds" and that "she" would need time to "re-compute." Methuselah didn't have the time she seemed to require to figure things out, so we asked some locals who were earnest in their wanting to help but, in the end, were even less helpful than our GPS. We decided to proceed on to Basalt Cellars in Clarkston, an hour's drive away, and find Merry Cellars on the way back to Spokane. We lost our way in Clarkston, getting us even farther behind schedule, especially by the time we'd finally arrived back within the Pullman city limits.

None of which, I suppose, should have surprised me, in that a week prior, having been faced with two alternative addresses for Merry Cellars, one of which, when called up by Google Map Imaging, only provided a visual of a lone mailbox at the edge of a very large and empty wheat field, I'd emailed Patrick Merry for clarification. He had assured me that the lone-mailbox locale was at the right address, the photo obviously just a really old one, in that there was now an industrial park on-site.

So, we arrived at Merry Cellars with no expectations of actually visiting that particular day, the day too far gone, but of merely pinpointing its locale so it would be less difficult for us to locate on our next time through.

As luck would have it, otherwise not in particular abundance for part of our day, we found an "OPEN" sign outside, and we made a beeline for the door, hoping to get through it before Patrick could get out, pull the sign inside, and lock up the premises for the evening.

We can thank our increasing good fortune in gaining such late-afternoon access not only to Washington State University Professor and Dean (College of Engineering and Architecture) Candis S. Claiborn, Ph.D., who had purchased several cases of Merry Cellars wine and was waiting for late-hour transport of them by her friend, John…but to the goodness-graciousness of Patrick Merry, Merry Cellars winemaker, who good-naturedly assured us that he'd much rather be there, talking wine with us, after hours, than at home, mowing his lawn (his other alternative).

What a turn to exceptional good luck it turned out to be for us! Not only because Professor Claiborn, the soon-to-arrive John, and Patrick, turned out to be such charming and knowledgeable tasting companions, but because Bonnie, Bruce, and I, had the opportunity to sample some truly magnificent wines that we, otherwise, would have had to put off doing until another day. In that last regard, there is no doubt in any of our minds (Professor Claiborn and John as enthusiastic about the Merry Cellars product as Patrick and we are), that this winery offers some of the very best wine in Washington State, having benefited tremendously from its young winemaker's philosophy that wine making should be "relaxed and minimalistic; showcasing varietal character and terroir, with only the best fruit treated as an expression of the vine, with avoidance of any trend toward over-processed, homogeneity." As for the winery's brochure articulating Merry Cellars' goal "to craft wines that are age-worthy, yet approachable—elegant, yet causal enough to be served at the family table," the Merry Cellars wines are certainly age-worthy, certainly elegant; and certainly sure to please any family member with the educated palate and nose to appreciate truly superb as opposed to merely mundane.

Every wine that Patrick brought out for our tasting enjoyment, beginning with his Sauvignon Blanc and Gewürztraminer, followed by his Syrah "Stillwater Creek," Cabernet Franc, Merlot "Stillwater Creek," "Mourvèdre" Syrah, Cabernet Sauvignon, and "Dolce Vita" dessert wine, had me insist he put a duplicate aside to take away with me. Besides which, I was persuaded by Professor Claiborn's enthusiasm (which I later concurred as well-warranted) to opt for bottles of un-tasted "Carménère," "Twilight Hills Red," and "Preoterre."

After an additional taste of Patrick's delicious "Dolce Vita," he confessed how it "just happened" as a result of his having once had an overabundance of blackberries at one and the same time as he'd had some excess Merlot on hand—a winning combination, as it turned out, to be sure.

When we all headed off for the evening, leaving Merry Cellars minus more than a few of its previous bottles of wine, and relieving Patrick of any lawn-mowing responsibilities, at least for the moment (way too dark), I couldn't help wonder at his revelation, heard at all three of the Palouse wineries, as regards the use of Hungarian oak barrels; Merry Cellars exclusively using fifty percent them and fifty percent American, no French. While I'm sure that there has to be more to the genuinely higher quality of product tasted in these three wineries than tasted in most of the samplings available just up the road a bit, in Spokane, there is no doubt in my mind that to miss the wines of this winery is to miss a highpoint of any wine-tasting tour of eastern Washington.

* * * * * * *

In our book *BACK OF THE BOAT GOURMET COOKING*, Bonnie and I recommended the following Merry Cellars to go with:

Jalapeño Poppers
Merry Cellars Gewürztraminer

Nachos
Merry Cellars Sauvignon Blanc

Pizza, Pesto
Merry Cellars Sauvignon Blanc

We've since come to discover that the Merry Hills "Carménère" can't be beat as accompaniment for our **Potatoes …for Stuffed Skins**; the Merry Hills "Preoterre" unbeatable compliment for grilled sirloin.

WAWAWAI CANYON WINERY (est. 2004)

5602 State Route 270
Pullman, Washington 99163
Telephone: (509) 338-4916
eMail: wines@wawawaicanyon.com
Website: www.wawawaicanyon.com

I-90 to Exit 279.

Merge onto US-195 S toward Colfax/Pullman.

Turn left at WA-270E.

Turn right at WA-270 E/Davis Way.

Turn right at N Grand Ave.

Turn left at SE Paradise St (signs for State Route 270E/WSU/Moscow.

Slight right at WA-270E/E Main St (signs for State Route 270/WSU/Moscow.

Continue to follow WA-270 E.

Destination will be on left.

Tasting Room Hours: 11-5:30 Thursday through Sunday, or call for appointment. Hours fluctuate in January and early February, due to weather, so be sure to call in advance.

HERE'S A WINERY whose products likely benefit tremendously from its own home-grown, many obscure, blending varietals—Petit Verdot, Malbec, Carménère, Lemberger... —used in its blends.

Even though most of the site's geographical surrounds often cool down early in the year to the point of debilitating frost, the microclimate of Wawawai Canyon is such that winds blow warm air up the Snake River and into the canyon for a tad more favorable grape-growing temperatures (the "lake" effect), that, at times, can match those of Red Mountain, one of central Washington's more famous premium growing regions. Helpful, too, for the production of big, powerful red wines, at/in Wawawai vineyards, are steep, south-facing twenty-to-twenty-three-degree vine-supporting slopes and marginal wind-blown loess. Often stressed to their limits, though, with growing seasons shorter than most other Washington areas, Wawawai Canyon grapes are usually harvested starting in August and completed by early October, the resulting smaller grapes tending to be more intense and more concentrated in flavor; vines discouraged by Mother Nature from creating a profusion of leaves in favor of fruit that betters the chances of the plant's successful propagation.

Wawawai Canyon Winery vines take up to five years before reaching adequate maturity for producing two tons of grapes per acre; most commercial vineyards, elsewhere in Washington, can yield three to five.

Here's a winery whose products benefit tremendously from its generosity in aging (its commercial reds, averaging two to three years in oak; its estate-bottled, ten years or more), especially in a state where the average Washington buyer seems intent upon having his wine from vine to barrel to bottle to table to belly in the shortest amount of time possible (most wineries out to cater to that buyer who's even reluctant to let a newly opened bottle of any red air for an hour or so, preferring to run the wine directly through an aerator).

Likewise, here's a winery whose products benefit tremendously from the passion of its winemakers, Ben Moffett and Christine Havens. "*Artigiano*—passion bottled," after all, gracing the lower right corner of each page of Wawawai Canyon's Winery's web site.

Ben's parents purchased the property in 1994 with the intent of starting a small organic farm, paying heed to the seller's bemoaning of a failed apple orchard and his voiced regret that he'd not "planted grape vines, instead." That same year, the Moffetts planted their first vines—Cabernet Sauvignon, Cabernet Franc, Syrah, and Sauvignon Blanc— and their learning process continued through experimentation benefited by friendship with nearby Lewiston, Idaho, viticulturalist Bob Wing. David and Stacia's son, Ben, expressed interest in wine and soon attended the newly opened School of Viticulture and Enology at Walla Walla Community College where he met Christine (a long-time food and wine devotee). By the same time the Moffetts finished construction of the Wawawai Canyon Winery facility, in 2004, Christine was ready to come on board as winemaker and partner.

A lot of additional experimentation took place after that initial 2004 vintage of eight barrels (200 cases). Grapes from early-immature vines often led to under-ripe vintages; all excellent groundwork upon which to build winemaking and recognize the properties of the fruit with which they were dealing. Eventually, they decided on the necessity of sourcing additional grapes from central Washington if they ever hoped to produce truly exceptional products. All of which paid off.

If we found its "Columbia Valley Fair Blend White" (lush flavors of pear, melon, honey floating atop mineral undertones) superb, and both its "Columbia Jazz Blend Red" (Malbec blended with Syrah), and three-year barrel-aged Sangiovese, some of the most complex and enjoyable wines we'd tasted in Washington…if we found its "Estate-Vineyard" Sauvignon Blanc a perfect complement for the picnic lunch we brought with us…if I was disappointed in its 100% "Walla Walla Carménère Rosé" (Bonnie and Bruce loved it)—possibly because I have an admitted bias against all rosé which I consider the usual result of indecisive winemakers unsure of whether to "go for" red or white—there's no denying that the tasting experience at Wawawai Canyon Winery was a joyous occasion, enhanced by Christine's obvious knowledge of wine, in general, and of her product, in particular, as well as by her overall unbounded enthusiasm which was genuinely infectious.

The tasting room, originally the milking parlor of an old barn, has been remodeled for perfect wine-enjoying ambiance that includes a Fine Art Gallery, highlighting local talent; the back section, with tables and chairs for casual dining, is charmingly rustic. (There are future plans for a gourmet restaurant).

If you've more time than a day, check beforehand to see what, if anything, is ongoing, as regards special events. A fall concert series often serves up an eclectic venue of folk, bluegrass, jazz, rock, Americana, even classical music. There are, also, seasonal barrel tastings, winemaker dinners, and "pairing parties" that team up Wawawai Canyon Winery wines with chocolate and/or cheese.

* * * * * * *

In our book *BACK OF THE BOAT GOURMET COOKING*, Bonnie and I recommended the following Wawawai Canyon Winery wine to go with:

Herb-Grilled Shrimp
Wawawai Canyon Winery Sangiovese

Ribs…Country
Wawawai Canyon Winery "Rosé"

CLARKSTON, WASHINGTON

THIS SOUTHERN WASHINGTON city is named after explorer William Clark, and sister city to just-across-the-Snake-River's Lewiston, Idaho, named after explorer Meriwether Lewis.

Located at the meet-up of the Snake and Clearwater rivers, in the Lewis-Clark Valley, some 465 river miles from the Pacific Ocean, it's at the head of the Columbia/Snake River navigation system and is part of the "Banana Belt," a decidedly temperate region because of its low elevation (731 feet above sea level), with year-round warm temperatures and mild winters.

Few people know, certainly I didn't, that the Lewiston-Clarkston Valley, like the area now around Lake Roosevelt (See Whitestone Winery) was a prime grape-growing and wine producing region over 100 years ago. Its first grapes were brought in by Frenchman Louis Delsol who, it was thought, initially passed through Lewiston in the late 1860s in search of gold but returned years later. More grapes were planted by Frenchman, Robert Schleicher, in 1872, after he mustered out of the US Army. It's believed that by 1900, he may have had over eighty acres of grapes in his vineyard. Last, but not least, German-born, Jacob

Schaefer arrived in the area in 1903, acquired one-hundred-sixty acres of land, and planted twenty acres of grapes in Clarkston where he built his winery. By the early 1900's, all three men were producing quality award-winning wines from over forty varieties.

All of which disappeared when most of the area voted itself "dry" even before official Prohibition.

CLARKSTON, WASHINGTON WINERY

BASALT CELLARS
(est. 2003)

906 Port Drive
Clarkston, WA 99403
Telephone: (509) 758-6442
E-mail: rick@basaltcellars.com or lynn@basaltcellars.com
Website: www.basaltcellars.com

I-90 to Exit #279.

Merge onto US-195 S toward Colfax/Pullman.

Turn right at US-195 S/State Route 195.

Continue to follow US-195S.

Entering Idaho

Continue on US-95 S.

Merge onto US-12 W via the ramp to Lewiston/Walla Walla.

Slight right at ID-128.

Turn right at ID-128 W/Down River Rd.

Continue to follow ID-128 W.

<u>Entering Washington</u>

Turn left to stay on ID-128 W.

Take 1st right onto Industrial and Recreational Rd/Port Dr.

Continue to follow Port Dr.

Destination will be on left.

Tasting Room Hours: 12-5 Wednesday through Saturday, or by appointment.

YOU DON'T NEED to look farther than the nearby hillsides to see the reason behind "basalt" being prominent in the name of this Clarkston, Washington, winery. Prehistoric volcanic activity has frosted the surrounding landscape with layer after layer of now long-cooled igneous stone.

On our way through the Basalt Cellars' front door (we'd lost our way), we passed the exiting country-western singer John Michael Montgomery (apparently performing somewhere locally)—or so informed the obviously star-struck Holly behind the tasting bar. Then, she proved herself the invariable diplomat by insisting, upon learning we were writing not one but two books, that her day was "full of celebrities." A very good start indeed, only made better, when Holly was sure that one of the Basalt Cellars' partners, Lynn DeVleming, would "insist upon stopping by to give us a personal hello," which, as it turned out, Lynn did and did.

And while I have to reserve higher praise for this area's Wawawai Canyon Winery and Merry Cellars, if just because I have an inherent tendency to think wineries with people fully devoted to wine, not merely looking upon it as a hobby, as well as ideally having a few home-grown grapes of their own to add to the mix, are the ones which produce the best wines, there's no denying that the partners involved in Basalt—Rick Wasem, chief Basalt winemaker and pharmacist (his Wasem's Drugs is the key retailer and home medical supplier for the whole Lewiston-Clarkston area), Don McQuary, and Lynn—still manage to produce some of the better wines, from central-Washington sourced grapes, that eastern Washington has to offer.

The three met up in enology classes at the Clarkston campus of the Walla Walla Community College, where they discovered themselves kindred spirits in their love of wine and in their emerging passion to get involved in winemaking. All of which resulted, 2004, in the production of the first 200 cases of Basalt Cellars wine. The winery has been going full-tilt ever since, our tasting venue, the afternoon we were there, including fifteen wines (eleven red, two white, one rosé, one dessert).

Of particular note, in that it so seldom occurred when tasting wine throughout Washington, Holly rinsed our glasses after our tasting of the whites (a Muscat Canelli, which was delicious, and a Sémillon which I liked but which Bonnie and Bruce didn't care for; did I mention Bonnie and Bruce like most everyone in the state, prefer reds?)...and before pouring the "Rosé."

The wine that turned out to be of most interest was the Merlot, because of its "nose" that enticed with strawberries and toasted marshmallow.

* * * * * * *

In our book *BACK OF THE BOAT GOURMET COOKING*, Bonnie and I recommended the following Basalt Cellars to go with:

Salmon...Cedar Plank
Basalt Cellars Merlot

Pico de Gallo
Basalt Cellars Muscat Canelli

OTHER OPINIONS

FOR ANYONE HEADED in the direction of the Spokane/Pullman, Washington, wine region, who would like to participate in wine-tasting, and would like input, other than my own, I recommend three internet sites of local wine-aficionados who can usually be counted upon to provide frequently updated timely reporting on what's going on wine-wise in the area:

DRINK NECTAR
www.facebook.com/sipofspokane#!/DrinkNectar

SIP OF SPOKANE
www.facebook.com/home.php?#!/sipofspokane

WINE TASTING REVIEWS
www.winetastingroomreviews.com/

INDEX

Arbor Crest Wine Cellars, 24
Barili Cellars, 31
Barrister Winery, 35
Basalt Cellars, 140
Caterina Winery, 41
Emvy Cellars, 46
Grande Ronde Cellars, 45
Knipprath Cellars, 51
Latah Creek Wine Cellars, 56
Liberty Lake Cellars, 62
Lone Canary Winery, 66
Masset Winery, 46
Merry Cellars, 126
Morrison Lane, 46
Mountain Dome Winery, 72
Nodland Cellars, 77
Overbluff Cellars, 83
Robert Karl Cellars, 89
Terranova Cellars, 106
Townshend Cellar, 109
Trezzi Wine, 114
Vintage Hill Cellars, 95

Wawawai Canyon Winery, 132
Whitestone Winery, 97

ABOUT THE AUTHOR

WILLIAM MALTESE is a long-time wine connoisseur, and author (with Bonnie Clark) of the bestselling *Back of the Boat Gourmet Cooking*, and (with Adrienne Z. Milligan) of the bestselling *The Gluten-Free Way: My Way*—both for the Borgo Press Imprint of Wildside Press. He's traveled much of the world, drinking good wine and eating good food at each and every opportunity. He has finally decided to put down some of his thoughts on fine wining and dining for THE TRAVELING GOURMAND series books for Wildside Press. He's also been honored with a listing in the prestigious *Who's Who in America*. For more information on William, please check out his websites:

www.williammaltese.com
www.facebook.com/williammaltese
www.facebook.com/flickerwarriors
www.facebook.com/draqual
www.myspace.com/williammaltese
www.myspace.com/flickerwarriors
www.myspace.com/draqual
www.myspace.com/maltesecandlegallery
www.theglutenfreewaymyway.com
www.mxi.myvoffice.com/williammaltese (Xoçai®)

www.ingramcontent.com/pod-product-compliance
Lightning Source LLC
LaVergne TN
LVHW041627070426
835507LV00008B/492